Gregory Gatserelia The Art of Interiors

Gregory Gatserelia
The Art of Interiors

Rizzoli New York

New York · Paris · London · Milan

Foreword by Patrick Perrin

I clearly remember the first time I met Gregory Gatserelia, an elegant, distinguished man. His kindness is blended with a great sense of organization and practicality.

Of Georgian origin, he grew up in Lebanon and Paris. He had a fundamental role in the creation of a new taste in Lebanese interiors, a mingling of West and East. He founded Beirut's first design gallery. This was the SMO Gallery, which took part in PAD Paris and PAD London on several occasions. And he laid the groundwork for a new wave of Lebanese designers. Since 2018 he has been a prominent member of the jury in Paris and London. His eclectic taste, unique spirit, and style make him noticed and admired among both collectors and gallerists.

As a great connoisseur and with a passion for design, he was a very close friend of Yves Gastou. This will hardly surprise anyone, since he too takes pleasure in inserting many art objects in his interior designs. But even more, he loves to conduct research, discovering and initiating new trends. Attentive to research and innovation, he masters the development of spaces by transforming them into warm, elegant, and unique places.

Meeting Gregory Gatserelia, this charming man with a free spirit, has proved a great opportunity for me. His taste has nurtured mine and enabled us all to discover the aesthetic and creative reality of his universe.

Patrick Perrin is the founder and CEO of the celebrated international PAD Design fairs.

Contents

Introduction
by Victor Gastou

Gregory is an explorer, a traveler in design, a unique person in the world of architecture. When he enters a gallery, the impression you get is of an adventurer who has just discovered the remains of some unknown civilization. It is firstly with his eye as an architect and a connoisseur that he observes and views the forms, the subtleties of a work. He scans the pieces in search of those small details that make it a creation apart. The elegance, the proportions of an artwork cannot be learned. There are no rules; it is a feeling, an intuition whispering to you that this object is beautiful. It is by following this intuition that Gregory is led toward an object and the discussions can begin. The architect then gives way to the passionate collector. I love the fact that he is so curious, so enthusiastic and passionate. Does he realize how rare it is to still feel desire, to still be so alive, after having seen and done so many things? His love of design stems from sensuousness. He loves volumes, shapes, materials. The decorative arts are discovered with the hand. We understand a sculpture by caressing it. It was this approach to beauty that brought us together. Objects, artworks, are made to be touched, handled, and shared. All this he knows only too well. He was one of the very first to share his knowledge with his clients. The relationships that he builds with them are remarkable. Without being assertive, he seeks to understand and inspire the people he guides. I like the way he adapts to the character and lifestyle of his clients. Some impose their dictates. He understands this and adapts his creations so that they best serve those for whom he works. Gregory always allows scope for eclecticism and originality in his interiors. It is always an honor to work with him and a pleasure to discover his latest creations.

Victor Gastou is the owner of Galerie Gastou and the son of the French collector, gallerist, and art dealer Yves Gastou.

An Essay
by Federica Sala

Federica Sala is an independent curator and design advisor. Formed in the design department of the Centre Pompidou, she lives in Milan, working over the years with institutions such as the Triennale di Milano and ADI Design Museum. She curates tailor-made projects or exhibitions for design and fashion brands and acts as art advisor to luxury hotels. She collaborates with Rizzoli and is editor-in-chief of *The Good Life Italia*.

A Designer Surrounded by a *Halo* of Legend

Gregory Gatserelia is a traveler gifted with an inquiring mind, an enthusiast, whose life and work, unlike many of his colleagues, are the subject of such mystery as to surround his production almost with a halo of legend.
Difficult to pigeonhole, Gatserelia is an authentic cosmopolitan who has come unscathed from the snares of that globalization that would have us all the same, when in reality every place has its own social rules and *genius loci*.
A Georgian by birth, he spent his childhood in Syria, where his father owned a manufacturing business. He left the country at the age of seven, when his father sent him and his brother to a boarding school in France. In 1967, following the coup d'état in Syria, his father lost everything, and the family moved to Lebanon, his mother's home. Here Gregory enrolled in the Académie Libanaise des Beaux-Arts. Ever since that fateful year, Lebanon and Beirut have received his unconditional love, not without shadows, but always with the power to call him back to them.

For this reason, reflecting on the editorial angle to give the book, together with Gregory and Joy Herro, his partner in crime to whom we owe this volume, it immediately became clear that the epicenter should be Beirut.
As a consequence, we are offering little more than scattered fragments of his early career in Canada, when, with his beloved brother Alexandre, he opened his first architectural practice, Gatserelia Design International, later merged with his present studio.

Gregory on *How High The Moon* by Shiro Kuramata, SMO Gallery Beirut (Lebanon), 2011

In dealing with these ten long and fruitful years, we have highlighted two night spots, *Acrobat* and *Boa*, which marked an epoch and dictated the rhythms of a generation.
In the same way, the volume presents a selection of the many international projects of residential or hospitality buildings that Gregory Gatserelia has designed over the years worldwide. We have preferred to guide readers to breathe the scent of the sea, as if they were walking on the Corniche and experiencing the hectic bustle of the city in the photographs by İeva Saudargaitė Douaihi interleaving the book.

Unlike many coffee-table books, this one is built around an autobiographical account enclosed in pink pages, accompanying us through the volume and its various sections, offering slices of the designer's life.
An authentic illustrated biography in images, it reveals Gregory's ties to Lebanon and Beirut, where we alight with a bird's-eye view, thanks to a map specially designed by the artist Tarek Abbar. Here the reader can identify the city's landmarks as well as the locations of the projects created by the studio—both residential and hospitality—explored in the book, selected from more than 100 projects completed over the years.

Project by Gregory, Manara, Beirut (Lebanon), 2015

Scrolling through the images of the homes Gregory designed immediately reveals, as Anne-Marie Habib stresses in the interview that opens the chapter, that contemporary art has always been not just a grand passion with Gregory. It is also a key to understanding the architect Gatserelia, a mentor and guide for many of his clients in nurturing or extending their interest and passion for contemporary art. Gregory Gatserelia has always combined his profession as an architect with that of art advisor, curator, talent scout, and promoter of the city's new generations, in art and design. This is recounted in the last section of the book, dealing with his role as a gallerist, in the interview with the artist Najla El Zein. It enables us to relive the epic years of the SMO Gallery, the forge of talents created by Gregory. From 2011 to 2018, he produced the works of many young artists, presenting them on the international market through exhibitions and participation in fairs, so helping ensure their success today.

Gregory's fascination is heightened by his becoming the supreme architect of Lebanese nightlife. Certainly not because he is a disco night owl. Those who know him also know how reserved and decidedly hip he is. Rather, for his flair in capturing the social moment and his ability to embody it in club and restaurant interiors that light up the nights. The second part of the book presents these hospitality projects. Working with the gaze of an anthropologist, over the years Gatserelia has come to grasp the needs of a continuously changing society, compelled to make resilience its banner, channeling vital energies into the celebration of conviviality, both domestic and public. His recipe, expertly dosed each time with different ingredients, with the eye of an alchemist rather than the architect's calipers, has created legendary places that have become the cradle of Lebanese society. Gatserelia knows how to indulge it and flatter it, but also mock it, creating venues in each case unique in style and consequently peerless. The unifying thread in his mutant style, as defined in the interview in the book with the artist Jacopo Foggini, with whom Gatserelia has worked widely in various countries, is a singular focus on embellishing ceilings, designed to give an important visual character to night spots or cues for conversation on evenings that struggle to take off and to encourage the shy. And it is precisely this aesthetic oxymoron that embodies all the strength and delicacy of a designer capable of lashing out but also, when needed, caressing to achieve a spatial balance.

Imagination

"How did I set my imagination working?
We were still living in a primitive place, without technological instruments. We found our happiness in action, friendship, games. We invented characters: we were knights, cowboys, supermen. We imagined conquests, invented love affairs. We felt close to nature and observed things carefully. Since I went to school in the countryside, I understood life cycle. We became aware of nature, of the birds building their nests and then laying their eggs. Sometimes we would help them: we would toss twigs close to them, so that they could pick them up easily. We began to make ourselves new worlds, saying to ourselves, 'I want to have a house here.' We built huts, at first on the ground, then in the trees, where we had our secret world. I had no access to the world outside my immediate setting, and I was far from my family, so I used to draw houses. I made up stories, I made up romances. I invented girlfriends I didn't have, who wrote me letters that I wrote myself. I would post the letter on Sunday nights when I was allowed to go out at the weekend, and I would receive it on Wednesday, reading it in front of my friends, as if it was from Eugénie or Sylvie, these were the fashionable names at the time. It was in this whole period that I felt the strength and passion to build up my own expression and character."

PORTRAIT OF GREGORY,
BEIRUT (LEBANON), 2015

Keen Eye

"My mother, of Lebanese origin, had an eye for beauty, and her gaze was different, quite unlike anyone else's. When I was a kid, she always kept pointing her finger—I have the same gesture—and saying, 'That's beautiful! That's good! That's interesting!' She kept pointing at whatever was beautiful. She couldn't always find words to express it, but she saw it. She always had a feeling for the good and the beautiful. She cooked wonderfully. She would make a sandwich with love, adding a sprig of some herb that made all the difference."

GREGORY, BEIRUT (LEBANON), 1970s

GREGORY WITH HIS MOTHER, BEIRUT (LEBANON), 1970s

GREGORY'S PARENTS, PARIS (FRANCE), 1960s

GREGORY, ON THE RIGHT, WITH HIS MOTHER AND BROTHER ALEXANDRE DURING A TRIP TO ROME (ITALY), 1958

Creativity

"My father was a lot like my brother, people who were parachuted into the wrong place. They were meant to land on some other planet! He was an extremely smart guy, a tech genius. He had a big factory in Syria in the 1950s. He was a good, brave, strong person. One day I'll write a book about him: an inventor, with a demanding character. He shaped me a little, giving me this sense of perfectionism. It's too bad he never had the luck or the means to push his research, but he made some inventions, and if they were feasible, they'd be extraordinary. I always feel my work is rather trifling compared to his. But I lack the ability to do what he was doing. I have no idea of physics or math. I was doing what I knew I could do while being as creative as possible."

GREGORY, ON THE LEFT, WITH HIS BROTHER ALEXANDRE, CHÂTEAU DE PROVEMONT BOARDING SCHOOL, ÉTRÉPAGNY (FRANCE), 1956

Separation

"It was difficult, it was too difficult. It was a wrench. Alex and I were deeply attached to my mother and this separation . . . My father had a heart of gold but he had a very harsh and old-fashioned idea of how to raise children. At the time, we were living in the Georgian community in Syria, close to his factory. Now, I understand that it was not a question of inheriting the culture, which was inconceivable for him. He wanted us to go to the very source. The most intellectual country, as my father saw it, was France.
It was hard because we were sent directly to a boarding school, very far away, in 1956, where a letter took three weeks to arrive. It was a sudden uprooting at the age of seven, in a world that was initially foreign."

Golden Beirut

"Before my father lost his fortune due to political conflict in Syria, we went to the best schools in France. When I arrived in Beirut in 1967, I discovered the most interesting city on earth. Those who knew Beirut before the war can understand what I'm saying. Others must have heard about it. This is the city where I have most relationships. I'm a good traveler. I haven't visited the whole world, but a large part of it. There are some continents that just don't interest me at all. They might have interested me a long time ago, but here everything is becoming shopping malls: through the ruins and the alleys, there are the big names. I love Lebanon because it has a history written in blood and drama and hope, by the beauty of the people, their resilience, their continuous struggle, their attachment. I can't express it, but I feel good. I'm proud of it. It's up-to-date, never off the pace. On the contrary, it's innovative."

GREGORY ON HIS HORSE, CLOSE TO BEIRUT RAFIC HARIRI INTERNATIONAL AIRPORT (LEBANON), 1970s.

Resilience

"Lebanon is historical attachment, lived experience, tragedy (almost like a Greek tragedy), a history of decline, of destruction, driven by the determination to erase it and promote other parts of the region. Because forty years ago, there was only Beirut and the desert. It was the city with the most important artistic expression, but unfortunately it was murdered, destroyed, ruined, violated. But what makes us become attached to this country is resilience. We're so attached to the country, to its culture."

GREGORY, ON THE RIGHT, WITH FRIENDS, BEIRUT (LEBANON), 1970s

GREGORY ON HIS ROWING BOAT, BEIRUT CORNICHE SEA (LEBANON), 1970s

GREGORY WITH THE BACKGROUND OF ZOUK POWER PLANT (LEBANON), 1970s

Multifaceted City

"In everyday life, everyone fought for their own Lebanon. This is because everyone has their own Lebanon. In wartime, everyone has their own Lebanon. In peacetime, everyone has their own Lebanon. My Lebanon isn't your Lebanon, it isn't his or her Lebanon. My battle isn't your battle."

GREGORY DESIGNING WINDOW DISPLAYS, BEIRUT (LEBANON), 1970s

Lebanese Talent

"What is my Lebanon? It's adoration for this country, which has had the worst shitshow possible. It had the third biggest explosion, the civil war lasting twenty years. They tried to kill it but nothing died. We keep going, we have the will to keep going. It is the only country in the world, despite its size and adversity, that creates so many talented people. The Lebanese. The Lebanese are talked about in every field: music, fashion, design, finance, art, architecture, cinema, cuisine. The country keeps turning out super talented people and making its mark."

GREGORY AT BEIRUT GARDENS BEFORE THE CIVIL WAR (LEBANON), 1970s

PP. 22-23: VIEW FROM HIGHEST ROOFTOP, ACHRAFIEH, BEIRUT (LEBANON), 2015

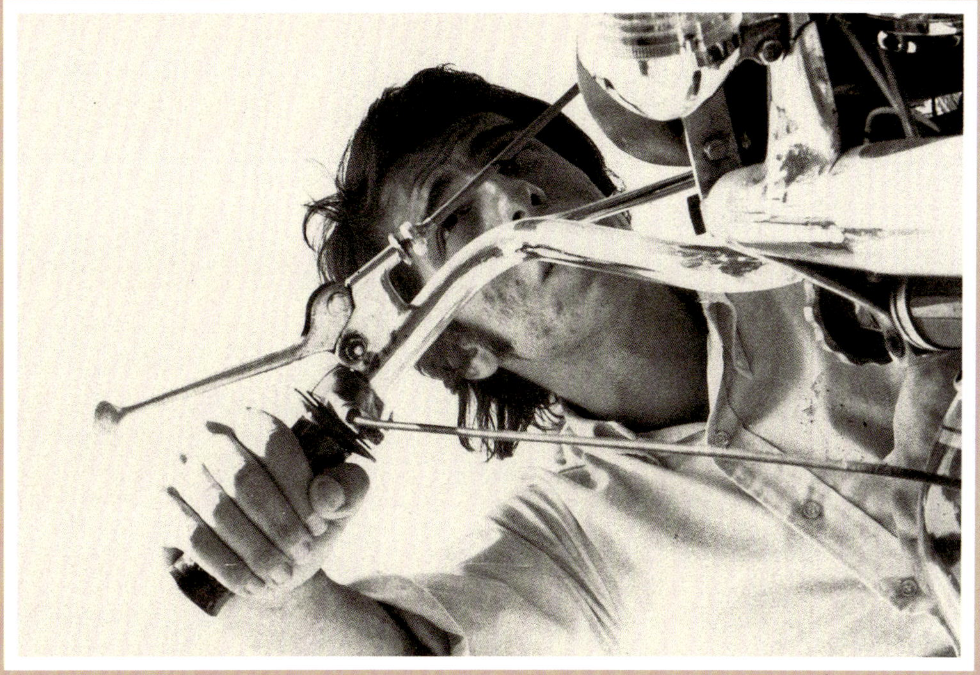

GREGORY ON HIS HONDA MOTORCYCLE, BEIRUT (LEBANON), 1970s

Joie de Vivre

"We don't think about the tragedies. We can't let others hear about them. In our flesh and blood, what makes us strong is the positives. I think of the beauty of the country, the motorcycle rides, the lunches in the small *boui boui* in the mountains, with the joie de vivre of the Lebanese, who are always partying as a way of expressing themselves. We work, then we party. We complain all day and in the evening we party. It's easy. There's the sea and the big city is close to the sea. I see my handyman, Abbas, on the weekend on his scooter in his swimsuit with two or three friends. They go to the beach and he smokes his *shisha*."

OPPOSITE: HOLIDAY INN HOTEL, SAINT GEORGES BAY, BEIRUT (LEBANON), 2019

Constant Evolution

"Beirut is always evolving. There's the Beirut of 1960-1961, then Beirut 1962-1963, then Beirut 1970. Beirut is always being turned upside down. You really have to go to the villages in the mountains to find some sort of continuity. Really to the villages that haven't been ravaged by war or hatred. There you can find the unchanging Lebanon. Otherwise it's always been Lebanon constantly changing its mentality."

HERITAGE BUILDING AND NEW CONSTRUCTION, MAR MKHAYEL, BEIRUT (LEBANON), 2018

In the Midst of Chaos

“The coast has changed, it’s become chaotic. We get a crazy pleasure in wanting to destroy this country aesthetically. We destroy our mountains, we tear them up . . . But in the end we accept it, we say, yes, chaos is part of our everyday lives, antennas, anything, we get used to it all, and we create our own nest. We frame our view, we plant something here so as not to see the horror there. But we’ve always fallen under its spell, and sometimes the outings to the mountains in the midst of nature reconcile us to the country.”

VIEW OF SEA AND MOUNTAINS NORTH OF BEIRUT, MAR MKHAYEL, BEIRUT (LEBANON), 2015

GREGORY ON HIS HARLEY-DAVIDSON MOTORCYCLE, SMO GALLERY BEIRUT (LEBANON), 2021

Motorcycle Passion

“To me, getting on a bike is already a thrill. I love all the motorcycles I have, the pleasure of choosing every morning which one to ride, whether for its physical appearance, the way it rides, or the sound it makes, whether it protects you or not, the way you feel the wind, the position you adopt. It’s about integration, the way you blend with the bike. Sometimes you’re sitting back with your legs pushed forward and sometimes you’re riding it like a horse. I love riding slowly just as much as I love riding fast. I ride roads and I’ve also done off-road (not much, as I’m not physically made for it). I like quiet off roads, without challenge. The advantage of Lebanon is you quickly reach the winding roads, the hairpin bends, not the highways. You get to places quickly, in no time you’re already in the mountains.”

My Rides

“My rides in Lebanon are mainly to discover the country. Wherever the country hasn’t been ravaged too badly, there are some fabulous places. You really need to make the effort to explore, and then find a place to have lunch! This is very important, because it’s the whole experience of exploring. It means associating the road with pleasure in the sense of smell, the wind, food, wine. Come back safe and sound, and always stay alert.”

GREGORY’S HELMET WITH BRONZE ANTS FOR “ROADS FOR LIFE” CHARITY, BEIRUT (LEBANON), 2018

GREGORY'S HOME NEIGHBORHOOD, SAIFI, IN BEIRUT CENTRAL DISTRICT, RECONSTRUCTED BY SOLIDERE AFTER THE CIVIL WAR, SAIFI, BEIRUT (LEBANON), 2017

My Neighborhood

"I live in a neighborhood that has been through everything, and now this neighborhood is without lights. That doesn't mean I love it any less. I've grown used to it. I saw all the things that happened, a neighborhood that I knew before the war, Place des Canons, no longer exists."

THOUGHTS

RAOUCHÉ, RAS BEIRUT, BEIRUT (LEBANON), 2017

La Corniche

“There was a time when I used to walk there every morning. This mixture of social classes, from the salesman to the politician to . . . everyone, all strolling about at 5 in the morning. I did it for four years, until the assassination of Prime Minister Hariri in an explosion. You start recognizing people. There was my friend’s father. Every time I saw him, I would switch sidewalks, because he walked so fast.”

Sporting Beach

“It hasn’t changed. It still has the feeling of the beaches we knew before the war. What’s extraordinary about Sporting is that it’s five minutes from the city center, it gives you a change of scenery, a place that feels like it’s in Greece, if you don’t look at the city. And you’re in a 1970s setting. It’s popular, but at the same time it’s the high society who goes there.”

SPORTING CLUB, BEIRUT (LEBANON) 2023

PP. 34-35: VIEW FROM GHOSTA OVER JOUNIEH BAY, GHOSTA (LEBANON), 2015

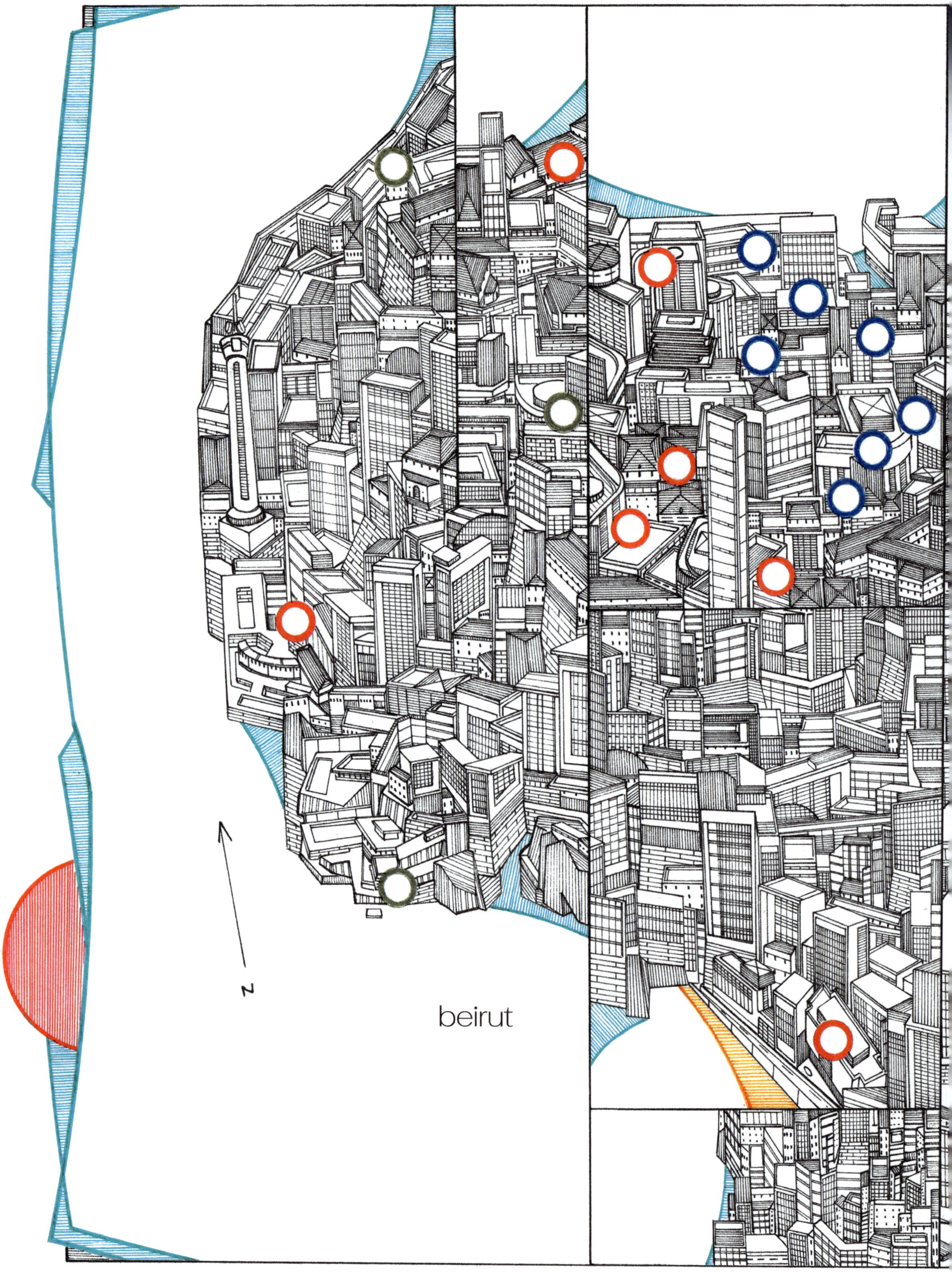
N
beirut

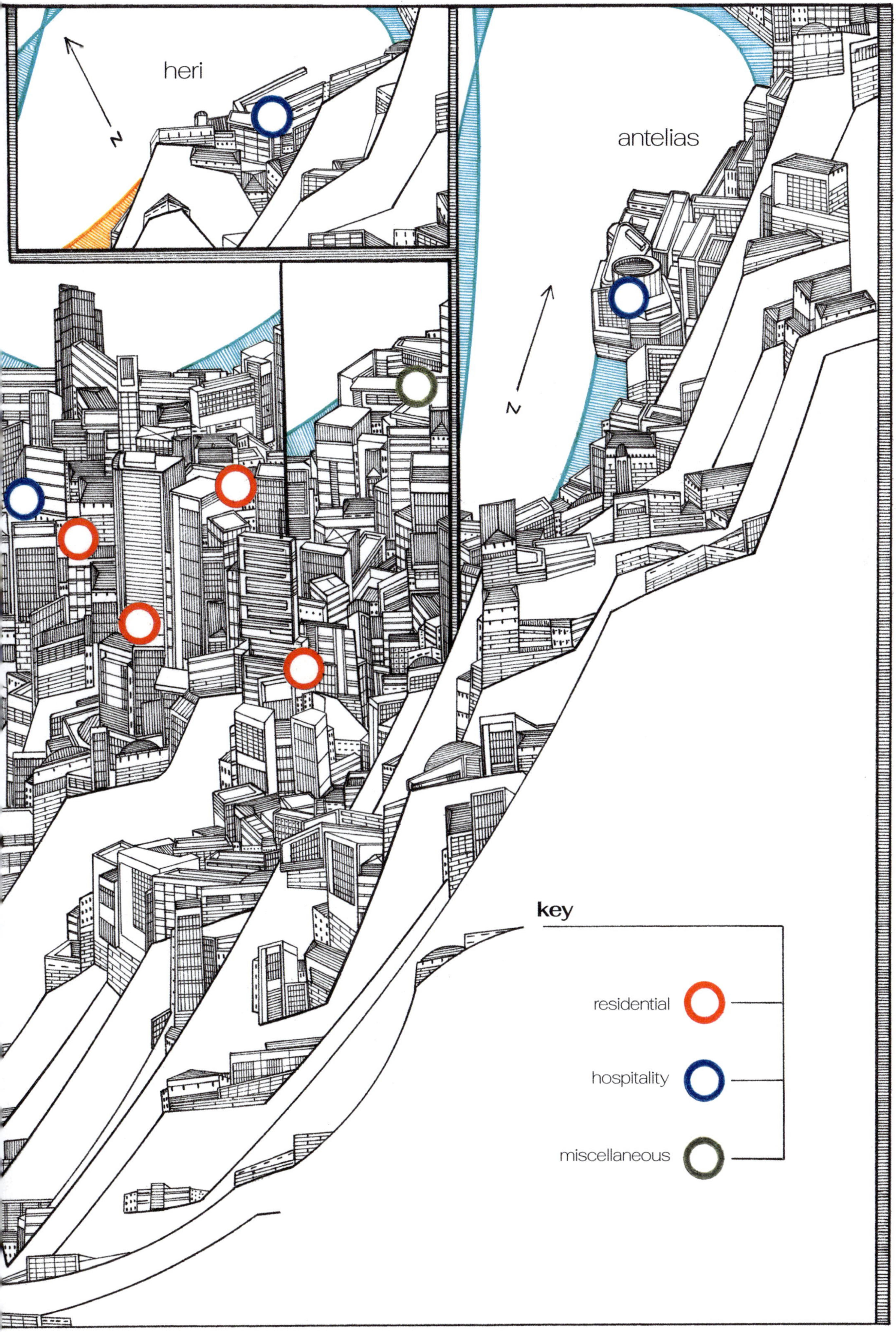

The map of Beirut with Gregory's view over the city. The pins point out the selection of residential and hospitality projects conceived by Gregory Gatserelia in Beirut and presented in this volume. Illustration by Tarek Abbar.

Project by Gregory, Downtown, Beirut (Lebanon), 2013

Residential Interiors

Gregory Gatserelia's work entails a meticulous, progressive process, an approach to design and to his client first and foremost, establishing a dialogue that often grows into a long-term relationship of esteem and friendship. He is always ready to listen to his clients' wishes and interpret their needs, which are often unexpressed, turning them into formal solutions that accompany those who will live in these spaces as they pass through the vicissitudes of life, in the ways they feel and present themselves to others. Often described as a mentor, a talent scout, he has played an essential role in bringing a contemporary and international dimension to Lebanon. Much of this is due to his deep knowledge of and ability to understand contemporary art, which he applies not for decorative purposes, but for the sake of the ambience that art can create in places and the emotions that it arouses.

A Conversation between Federica Sala and Anne-Marie Habib

Anne-Marie Habib is a consultant nephrologist of mixed background, with a Lebanese father and a Swiss mother. She grew up in Lebanon but became a citizen of the world soon after earning a degree in medicine. She lived and worked in New York and London, before settling down in Monaco, her current home.

An Eye on Contemporary Art

FEDERICA SALA You've known Gregory for many years, and you've commissioned him to create several interior projects in very different parts of the world. How did you first meet, and how has your relationship with him developed over time?

ANNE-MARIE HABIB I first met Gregory through a mutual friend who was already a client of his and who introduced us to him soon after we bought our apartment in the Sursok neighborhood in Beirut. My husband and I were immediately inspired by Gregory as a person. He came across as being sensitive, gentle and, at the same time, experienced. One could tell from the start that he was passionate about art and interior design.
I later realised that my parents had already known him, when he was much younger and about to leave for Canada to start his career. Together with his brother Alexandre, he had rented a chalet in a ski resort that belonged to my father. He had refurbished the chalet wonderfully, to the point that all the following tenants did not want to make any changes. He already showed great talent, despite having very little means offered to him.
At the time we wanted to change the style of our home, which was classical, giving it a contemporary feel that was completely new to me. So it was Gregory who introduced me to all that. We instantly became close friends. Ours is a genuine friendship that we still cherish today. But our meetings with Gregory were very professional. His insight into design was a real eye-opener for us. My husband and I were both very busy with our jobs, so we didn't have a lot of time, and Gregory was a sort of mentor who helped us approach the world of contemporary art. It was a world that intrigued us, but about which we knew very little. Gregory talked more about art than ornamentation. It was about much more than decorating the house. We started going to galleries together, like Thaddaeus Ropac's in Paris. He, too, became a friend of ours. Gregory taught me how to appreciate different kinds of art by going to museums and visiting galleries together. He guided me toward some excellent artists, both well-established figures and emerging ones, including Robert Longo, Alex Katz, Anselm Kiefer, and Antony Gormley. Listening to their stories and entering that world got me interested in new things.

FS What is your relationship with Gregory like?

A-MH He was my mentor. But what I love about Gregory is not just his interest in contemporary art, but the fact that he truly has an eye for things, and that he knows a great deal. And in spite of this, he's very modest. In fields like these you meet lots of people who think they know everything. Gregory never acts like that; he's always ready to take a step back. One of the things that makes him so good is that he can grasp the client's style instead of pushing his own. It's very pleasant to work with him; he listens and adapts to your wishes. Interior design is a modern, fast-paced industry requiring many talents and learned skills. Greg was up to this challenge. Trends come and go; Greg manages to stay ahead of the curve. He has never ceased doing the research, keeping up-to-date. Even though he has many more skills and is much more knowledgeable and cultured than others, he always expresses the curiosity of someone who wants to explore new things. You might say he does his own homework! He conducts extensive research into the artist's work, in an academic way. This is what differentiates him from other architects. He goes further. That's what has always impressed me. He has a strong work ethic and a deep passion for the craft. He has an eye for detail, a natural understanding of colors and intuition about space, harmony, and balance.

FS Apart from the visit to Ropac's gallery in Paris, have you ever taken any other trips together?

A-MH We have often traveled together, because Gregory is a lot of fun and is an enjoyable person to spend time with. More than once we've visited Art Basel together, but never for the purpose of decorating a home, always in search of an atmosphere. And this is also the real difference in his approach to interior design. Often, when you enter a home designed by an architect, you see their distinctive imprint, even more than that of the owners themselves. This never happens with Gregory because he doesn't have his own style; rather, he always creates an atmosphere. He is ingenious and innovative. We have since decorated two other houses with him and they are all completely different in style and design. He has taken into consideration the locations (New York and Monaco) and the space.

FS How does Gregory relate to art?

A-MH Gregory is himself an artist. He has the soul of an artist. He designs beautiful furniture pieces and has done so since he settled in Milan, where he met several skilled artisans. He has made us a neon, which we have at the entrance in our home in Monaco, and a bar, both a great addition. His work reflects his personality; it sums up everything I appreciate about him: his human and intellectual qualities, his creativity, and his passion.

Art collection curated by Gregory, Beirut (Lebanon), 2009

L'ART

L'univers des ORIENTALISTES
Paris
ART

Van Gogh
ziad antar
expired

MONET
Architecture in the 20th Century
PIANO

BANKSY
BANKSY YOU ARE AN ACCEPTABLE LEVEL OF THREAT

Contemporary Art

“Contemporary art starts from the moment a human being, a kid, starts doodling, expressing their thoughts. That’s contemporary art, and we naturally express ourselves depending on how we feel and view things. The problem of academic art is that we try to conform to rules that are extraordinary, but not natural to our reflexes, nor to our primitive and expressive and natural language. It’s conditioned by a technique. While a baby’s art, a kid’s art, is spontaneous. It expresses what they feel. If you manage to prolong this—which is difficult because we’re full of mannerism—with the addition of intellect, it becomes the expression of beautiful contemporary art.”

GREGORY WITH HIS 3D MODELS, BEIRUT (LEBANON), 1970s

BEST OF

Louis Vuitton
THE FASHION BOOK

SUN
SET

GREGORY AT SMO GALLERY, BEIRUT (LEBANON), 2013

Collectors in Space-Time

“A collector is someone who’s passionate. I’ve created ‘collectors in space-time.’ They were collectors for the duration of their project. After that, did they continue their collections? I don’t know! I don’t have clients who have continued to buy on their own, clients with the souls of collectors. Others have bought enough for their homes. But sometimes they turn up, they come back, years later, saying: ‘Ah Greg! We want such-and-such an artist!’”

UCCELLATI

Lily's, Beirut (Lebanon), 2017

Hospitality Interiors

Anyone who has ever been to Lebanon, and in particular to Beirut, has likely been inside a nightclub or restaurant designed by Gregory Gatserelia. Over the years, his taste and versatility in design—which lets you glimpse a subtle common thread linking the projects, but won't let you label them a priori—have helped him to create some of the most famous places where locals in high society get together. *Cocteau, Seray, Kampaï, Sultan Brahim, L'Ancien Capitole*. Places in whose rooms the crème de la crème of Lebanese society gather, forge personal relationships, and sign off big business deals. But these are also the places of endless Beirut nights spent dancing on the tables of *Crystal* or *Spine*. Because in Beirut, going out at night is perhaps the only way to truly get to know the city and its people.

A Conversation between Federica Sala and Jacopo Foggini

As a child in the family factory in Turin, Jacopo Foggini discovered the versatile nature of methacrylate and polycarbonate, commonly used in the automotive industry. Fascinated by their aesthetic and chromatic features, he started creating works of art and installations all over the world, collaborating with important international design and architectural firms.

A Mutating Style

FEDERICA SALA I know you've been acquainted with Gregory for many years and that you often collaborate on his projects, interior ones but above all those related to hospitality: bars, restaurants, clubs, hotels. What took me by surprise when I saw the many hospitality projects he created in Lebanon, many of which included your site-specific installations, is the constant change in register among them. Almost as if they weren't even made by the same person. What's it like to work with Gregory?

JACOPO FOGGINI I consider Gregory a star who's hard to classify as compared with many other architects who are a part of our world. What I like about him is his versatility: his projects are always completely different, they never resemble one another. And this is rather unique, because usually, when architects find a language that the public understands, they carry it forward and apply it so that their projects are instantly recognizable. On the contrary, Gregory always questions himself, and this is why his interiors never resemble one another. His style is a completely mutating one, but at the same time he maintains a certain transversal classical look even if the venues change, the elements change, and the projects are very different.

FS What's Gregory's relationship with other artists like?

JF Gregory is someone who delves deep into his relationship with artists and designers. I have a truly special relationship with him, not just one of friendship or esteem—we have a real chemistry between us. This leads to our having a diverse creative exchange, one that goes beyond the usual request that artists receive to interpret a vision. When you work with Gregory—although I'm not sure the same thing happens with others, but it does with me—the relationship is characterized by total mutual esteem, a sort of love. You advance courteously, respectful of other people's ideas. This is very different from what usually happens, in other words, when we artists/designers are called at the last minute to give some strength to projects that have already been conceived. With Gregory it's not like that, the work starts from the very beginning, like planting a seedling and watching it grow, watering it day after day together. And Joy's role is also crucial. Joy Herro is Gregory's other half, a designer and design advisor who was also his partner in crime in The Great Design Disaster (see p. 226). Joy has a freshness, a sharpness, and a rare intelligence, especially because she is a very young woman. For Gregory the research is extremely important. He often accompanies his private clients in their purchase of artworks and design, both contemporary and historical, and for this part of his work Joy's contribution and taste have become a very important resource, because she has put a whole series of new colors and new nuances in his already multicolored palette.

FS Talk to me about Gregory's Beirut.

JF As you know, Gregory worked a lot in the United Arab Emirates and in Lebanon before being deservingly recognized in Europe as well, but his ties to Beirut are special. I've seen lots of the works he made there. Much of the center of

Amar Café, Downtown, Beirut (Lebanon), 2020

Beirut was designed by him, from *Spine* at the top of a skyscraper, to all the clubs and restaurants in the central area, from the first Japanese places, to *Amar*. The latter location, which we worked on together, was the winner of the Best Project for Middle East Asia.

FS How important was Gregory's work for the nights in Beirut?

JF There's a great fervor in Beirut. The people here need to express themselves because they're living in a place where the tension is always high. This is why young people want to go out all the time, and the Beirut nights are famous because you find yourself in situations that only exist in this particular city. I remember a concert one evening by a singer in what was once a mattress factory. There were armed guards outside and suddenly you heard the voice of a nightingale rising up inside a crazed bunker of techno music. Beirut is a city of contrasts, and Gregory has always known how to capture them. For instance, at the *Spine*, which is located, as I told you before, on the rooftop of a skyscraper, Gregory had the idea of using the lighting to create a sort of open-air cage of lights. So, instead of creating a dance floor he turned the architecture itself into the venue's entertainment, building tables to dance on. It's a place I've been to lots of times and where I'm always happy to return.

Social Parameters

"There are very precise and decisive parameters for creating interiors that will please the Lebanese. Especially for the commissions I receive, because I'm labeled a high-end designer, so I have to attract the Beirut upper crust. And these people only feel good, only express themselves in keeping with the parameters I adopt. They all need to be in the limelight. They put on a big act. If they go out to lunch, it's to network, to make contacts with professionals. There are women's lunches that have from eight to twenty people sometimes. The atmosphere at lunch is noisy, but in the evening it's a little quieter. The spirit of community is very important, without people really knowing one another, just knowing one another by sight: I was one of the first, if not *the* first, who didn't put in a dance floor. It was in my *Crystal* project. It changed the mentality in nightclubs. People would dance on the tables. As to Toronto, *Boa* was a small bar, transformed into an iconic location, where all the DJs regularly played. It broke the rules; the codes were to stop the music at 1 a.m., but there the music lasted until 3 to 4 a.m. We were the first to host gay nights in Toronto."

BOA CAFÉ BY GREGORY AND HIS BROTHER ALEXANDRE, TORONTO (CANADA), 1989

THE SWIMMING POOL BY GREGORY AND HIS BROTHER ALEXANDRE, TORONTO (CANADA), 1994

ACROBAT BY GREGORY AND HIS BROTHER ALEXANDRE, TORONTO (CANADA), 1989

ACROBAT CAFÉ SKETCH BY GREGORY, TORONTO (CANADA), 1989

[…] "We wanted *Boa* to be sensual but undefined. We wanted to make a statement about contemporary culture and how we spend our leisure time." Indeed, the café is suffused with the current cultural vogue for the assimilation of the once well-defined categories of high and low art. […]

From an article by Mayer Rus (*Interior Design* magazine, 1991)

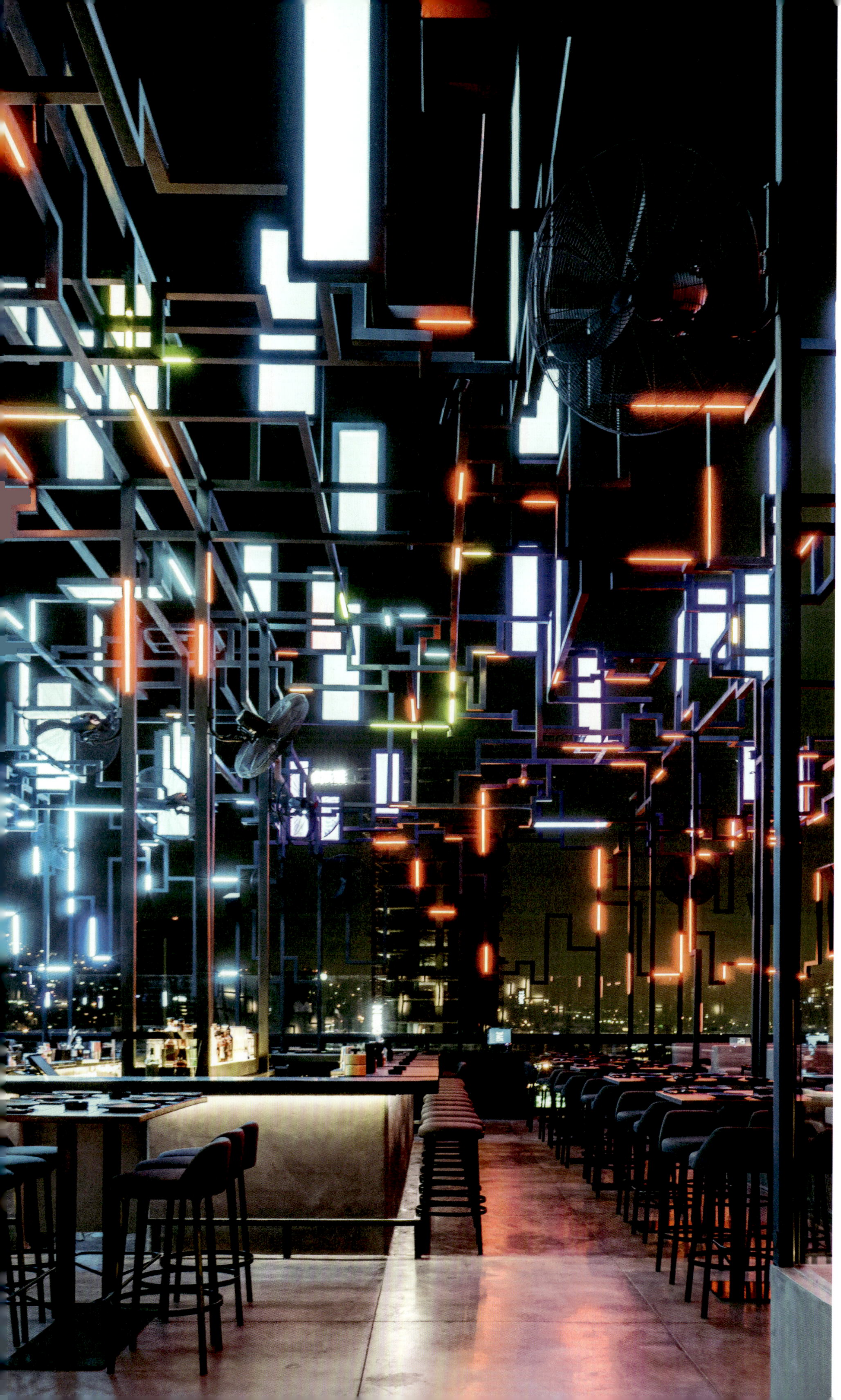

VIVRE

The Art of Decorative Ceilings

Gregory Gatserelia clearly has in mind the parameters to follow if you want to design a place that will be to the liking of the Lebanese, and especially if the project involves designing something for the local jet-set. For Gregory, everything starts not from the entrance but from the moment a person arrives. Where does the car stop? What do people see as soon as they get out of the car? How are they introduced to the venue? And so, step by step, he rolls out his "red carpet," made up of different elements each time but that instantly creates that feeling of being at the heart of the scene.
The room inside should preferably be square–better for it not to be rectangular–if it is to allow everyone to have a table that is of equal importance, a stage on which to be seen and look around. Walls and dividers are out, because in Lebanon you don't go out looking for intimacy. Quite the contrary. Here you go out in large groups to see and meet others. No small rooms and tiny corners; everyone has to be out in the open. But emerging from behind the architect is the man Gregory Gatserelia, reserved and level-headed, paradoxically far removed from the exuberance that his venues have cleverly succeeded in stimulating. And the reserved side of this man can be found in the visual poetry of the ceilings, perhaps the only real signature style in Gatserelia's hospitality projects. Because the ceilings in the places he designs are filled with ideas, allowing us, he says, to have a place to look at if the conversation lags, an escape route of sorts. From the metal coffered ceiling with geometric shapes of *Seray*, to the sinuous lines branching out from a single center, as if to hypnotize us, at *Lily's*, the ceiling is quite often one of the key elements of the project. At *Society* you can't help but notice the large-scale ceiling sculptures: brass circles that are both lighting elements and the creators of the mysterious shadow play on the ceiling. Or the incredible installation of glass grapes made for the wine bar ceiling by Lara Khoury and produced in a small Syrian village just before the war broke out.
But there's also Jacopo Foggini's *Nuvola* for the ceiling of the *Amar*. It's his attention to detail and unprecedented ability to open up new points of view that have become Gatserelia hallmarks since his historic *Balthus*, *Celcius*, and *Le Cocteau*.

For Me chair by Gregory for SMO Gallery Beirut, 2016

Art & Design

Interior architect, designer, art dealer, collector, but also mentor and talent scout. Gregory Gatserelia is notable for his passion for design, art, and architecture, as well as craftsmanship. Never repetitive but not necessarily cutting-edge, Gatserelia began doing art design even before the term existed. With his SMO Gallery he laid the foundations for the Lebanese *nouvelle vague* of artists and designers, a generation that has capitalized on his teachings and managed to revive local production. Today, with The Great Design Disaster (see p. 226), he is lavishing attention on detail and conducting constant research in the spirit typical of all his projects.

A Conversation between Federica Sala and Najla El Zein

Najla El Zein's artworks explore the relationship between form, use, and space. Born in Beirut in 1983, El Zein moved to Paris at the age of two. She studied at the École Camondo, receiving a BA in Product Design and an MA in Interior Architecture and Spatial Design. After graduating, she worked in the Netherlands and then relocated to Beirut in 2011. Coinciding with the 2022 FIFA World Cup, El Zein was invited by the Qatar Museum to provide works for two public spaces in Doha. Her art has been exhibited at numerous public institutions, including the Dallas Museum of Art's exhibition *Women + Design: New Works* (2018–19). El Zein's pieces have been acquired for the permanent collections of museums such as the Dallas Museum of Art, TX, and the Victoria & Albert Museum, London. She lives and works in Amsterdam, the Netherlands.

Sowing Seeds

FEDERICA SALA There are very few images of SMO Gallery, since smartphones didn't exist back then. This means that the vital role that the gallery and its activity played in Beirut, and for all the Lebanese artists of that generation, lives on only in the stories told by those who had that experience. What was your relationship with the gallery like?

NAJLA EL ZEIN I had just arrived in Beirut and those were the years when the gallery was being set up. At the time, I was doing different jobs: from stage sets to store window displays, but merchandising, too. I was training to be an artist, and my encounter with the country I was born in, but a place I had never lived, was of key importance for my discovery of the local artisanal production. Gregory had a large collection of his own, but he had opened this gallery for the purpose of offering a space to many talented young Lebanese artists, editing their works. Meeting him gave me a great feeling of relief. I was trying to find my way forward as an artist, and seeing a man who was both a dreamer and ambitious at the same time, who had confidence in me from the moment we met, gave me the peace of mind I needed to be able to express myself without fear. I developed my *Nuages*, which I was already working on, but always for a temporary context, while Gregory gave me the chance to take the project to a permanent level. I needed to lay the groundwork for myself, and by representing me as an art dealer, he gave me the chance to nurture my art.

FS What was it like for you and for the city in general to participate in the opening of SMO?

NEZ At the time, there was a lot of energy in the city, which was starting to get back on its feet. There were lots of artists and designers who were setting up small but exciting and meaningful projects. SMO Gallery was the means that allowed everyone to grow, to have a more official role, to channel all the energy and thus make it more stable. Gregory had shown his personal collection, but at the same time he had organized one of the first art and design shows in Beirut. The gallery succeeded in perfectly capturing that moment in the city, its people, and the very soul of Beirut nights. Imagine the emotion an artist might feel at having a gallery decide to invest in their production, with full respect and freedom, and with no strings attached.

FS Can we say, then, that SMO Gallery contributed to your career?

NEZ Absolutely. Gregory had decided to take part in the first edition of the Design Days in Dubai, and for that occasion the gallery produced many works. Among them, the installation that allowed me to make a name for myself: it was a luminous sculpture called *6302 Spoons*. This wouldn't have been possible if Gregory hadn't been behind the project and hadn't supported me. We began participating in the PADs, in Paris but also in London. But, most importantly, because Gregory is an interior architect, we started working on some site-specific pieces for his projects. For instance, for an apartment in the Platinum Tower in Beirut, we created an interactive installation that we called *Breathing Wall*: it consisted of a wall that was transformed as the day went by thanks to a complex motorized system. It took me months

Installation *Breathing Wall*, Najla El Zein, 2013

to finish the project and Gregory's support during that time was crucial.

FS Do you think that the activity of SMO Gallery was a natural offshoot of his sincere passion for art and design?

NEZ Gregory was definitely the one who gave an initial push to the birth of the art and design milieu in Beirut. He put together an extremely heterogeneous group of artists, ones who were not fossilized in the concept of a single movement together, but were rather each of them free to express themselves however they wished. Many of the artists that he presented went on to be successful in their work. He also deserves credit for opening up the local scene to others. After SMO, other galleries opened up nearby and this played a fundamental role for the city in general and for the quarter in particular. Before the SMO Gallery there was nothing in that area. He deserves all the credit for sowing the seeds.

SMO Gallery Beirut at PAD London, 2013

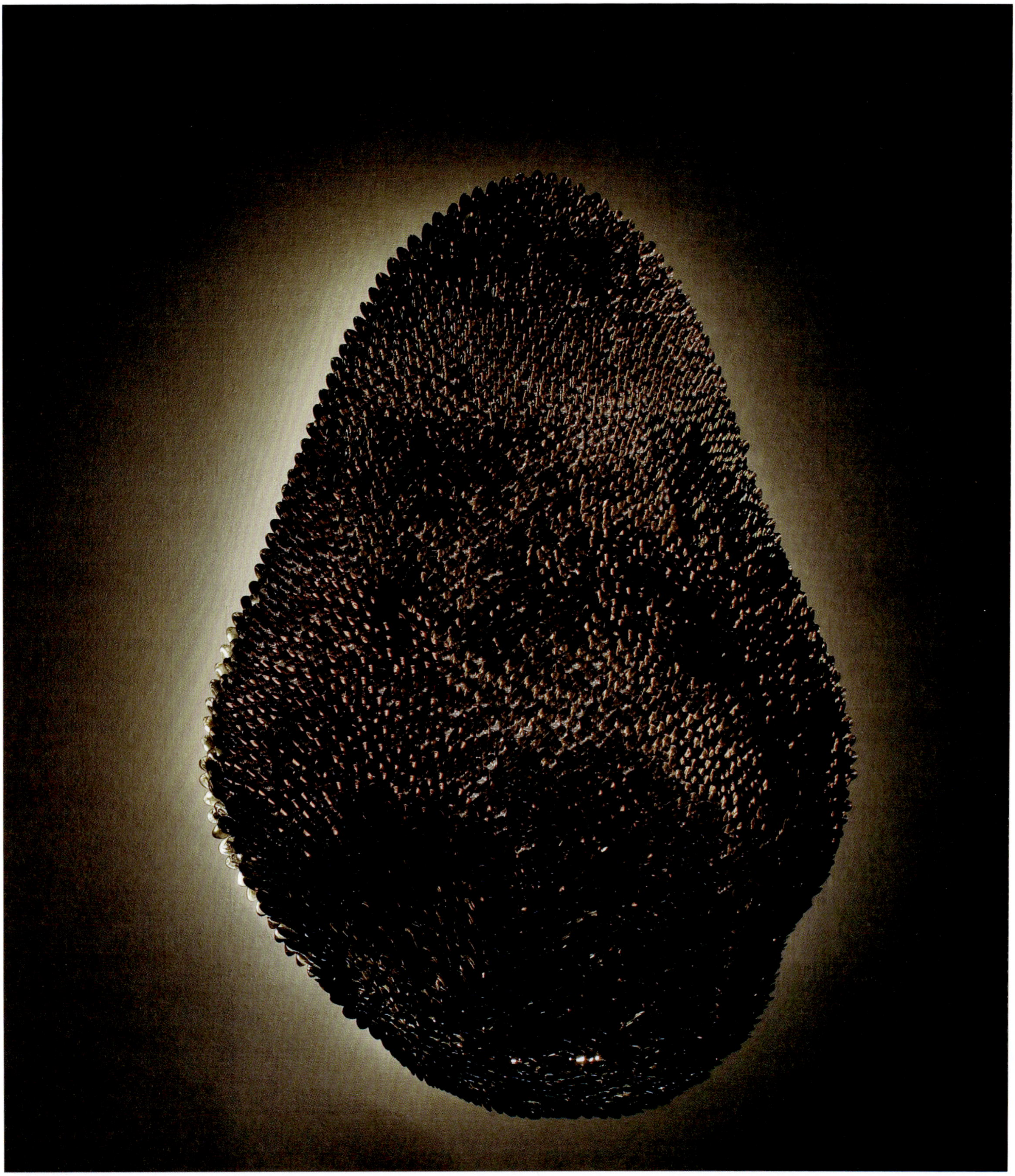

6302 Spoons by Najla El Zein for SMO Gallery Beirut at PAD Paris, 2014

The SMO Gallery

Opening of the exhibition *Piètement de Banc* at SMO Gallery Beirut, November 2012

The SMO Gallery was both a personal and collective adventure that became a milestone in the city's history. Many of today's great Lebanese artists and designers were inspired to measure up to it, and it launched their careers. It opened in 2011 on Senegal Street, in the Karantina quarter in northeast Beirut, a district where the abattoirs used to exist and few people cared to venture. The gallery began as a sort of repository for showing clients the collection of pieces Gregory had purchased, including some that other clients had turned down but he had been unwilling to lose: Ettore Sottsass, Hella Jongerius, Andrea Branzi, Alessandro Mendini . . . The "repository" was soon transformed into an exhibition space to give design students the opportunity to see these collectibles firsthand. And it was then that Gregory decided to help them produce their first works, to launch them on the market thanks to preview-night dinners with famous chefs and table settings that have become legendary. The fame of the gallery was immediate, and the first international exhibitions soon arrived: the first edition of the Design Days in Dubai and the PAD in London and Paris. It was an adventure that ended in 2018, when Gregory decided once more to devote himself only to interior design projects, and it set the tone for the city, the neighborhood, and a new generation of artists.

An Accidental Adventure

"The SMO Gallery adventure was accidental. I had a great collection that I'd acquired, not for the sake of acquiring it but so as not to let go of the beautiful pieces when I was faced with the wrong-headedness of my clients. When I presented some beautiful pieces, the clients failed to turn up. I was pulling the trigger. I didn't want to lose the items so I bought them. And little by little, I built up my collection. At one point, I was looking for a place to store my collection, and that's when I discovered the SMO premises, which were divided into separate compartments. And little by little, the owner said to me, 'Ah, you can take over a bit more space because the lease of the sandwich seller is coming to an end, so you can take over his place.' In this way I expanded. Then he offered me his corner where he stored his things. He offered it cheaply. And I ended up taking over the whole place. Once I'd demolished the walls, I found myself with a beautiful space! SMO! And then I thought: 'I'm going to display my pieces, and I'll set aside a small budget for students who can't travel.'"

SMO GALLERY BEIRUT AT PAD PARIS, 2014

Growing Talents

"I had Ettore Sottsass, Alessandro Mendini, Andrea Branzi, Oscar Niemeyer, Hella Jongerius. I had lots . . . lots . . . lots of pieces, Bořek Šipek, and paintings, and so on. After that, when people heard I was setting up a gallery, I was contacted by designers who wanted to show off their things. This is where I came up with the idea of discovering young Lebanese talent. Word got around and so I had a lot of contacts and I made a selection. I immediately spotted Najla El Zein. And I started doing personal projects with these artists. Most of them eventually made their names. They're all somewhere, they've gone on. It gave them a chance to show off their work."

DINNER ON THE OCCASION OF AN EXHIBITION OPENING AT SMO GALLERY BEIRUT (LEBANON), 2011

BANC DES AMOUREUX BY ZIAD ANTAR FOR SMO GALLERY BEIRUT (LEBANON), 2012

Universal Style

"Being Lebanese, because of the Lebanese diaspora caused by the war, with people growing up elsewhere, means being educated internationally. These designers are not in the least the expression of the region, or barely. These are people who think and express themselves internationally. There's nothing Lebanese about them. Even Khaled El Mays isn't Lebanese. He's primitive, brutalist. david/nicolas are not Lebanese. I like their sincerity. They're people of their generation. They want to achieve a universal expression not a traditional one."

TGDD

The Great Design Disaster is the project, revolutionary in terms of its commercial mechanism, launched by Gregory Gatserelia together with Joy Herro in 2019. It is a formula that puts the collectors themselves at the center of the creative process. In this way they find themselves for the first time emerging from the usual logic of acquisition by creating one-off pieces, expertly orchestrated by the two creatives and developed by a network of outstanding craftworkers. The production is wholly Italian, and for this reason the couple is resident for part of its time in Milan, keeping a close eye on every phase of the work together with their international clientele. As Gregory observes, "Life is made up of encounters. Projects never arise by chance, but always thanks to the meetings between people that we encounter along our way, finding affinities, a shared sensibility. And so it was with Joy. I immediately found

TGDD workshop visit at VIMAS upholsterer, Palazzolo sull'Oglio (Italy), 2020

Sketch by Gregory for TGDD, Milan (Italy), 2023

myself attuned to the care and attention she brought to the details, to the work of the craftsmen. At first she oversaw the making of my pieces, but then she gradually opened my spirit to new materials, so guiding me from more natural materials to include synthetics and, more generally, to experiments with a broader range. Until at last we came up with this subversive idea of reversing the process of acquisition, often based only on the commercial and historical value of a piece rather than desire and the production process." In this way collectors find themselves guided by their feelings, giving rise to something that did not exist, and are led, perhaps in rather bohemian ways, to celebrate the lyrical sense of the home, giving new connotations to the terms of uniqueness and exclusivity that usually apply to the search for collectibles. So this is an all-encompassing experience, without the pressure of time but with pleasure in every stage of the journey through repeated visits to craft workshops to foreground their value, their heroic ability to transform materials, and knowing how to lead them wherever the collector's desire means to take them. An approach that has the flavor of seduction,

TGDD workshop visit at Fonderia Battaglia, Milan (Italy), 2020

that celebrates the wonder that comes from making, revealing all the intelligence and sense of humor of those behind it and who, accustomed to traveling with important clients, have found a new region to explore with collectors. Hence The Great Design Disaster is not a collection but a path, with the focus on human relationships: between the collector and the agents, but also between the client and the craftworkers.

And the whole process is seasoned with food, with the pleasure of consuming it together, as the events they organize show clearly: moments that celebrate the passion for people and the earthly things of life. Like the *Post Disaster Room* conceived for the Menart Fair at the Fondation Boghossian in Brussels, or the project on the trattorias of craftworkers presented in Milan at the last Fuorisalone. With the focus not so much on the process as on the feelings behind the creation.

The Adventure with Joy

"I'm interested in the whole adventure, because it's about Joy, because it revolves around Joy. She runs everything. I don't want to get involved. She asks my opinion and I say: 'Do as you like!' So far, she's done a great job, which is reassuring!"

"Rock bands only look great in their teens! They fade away as they get older. I love the idea of Daft Punk! We don't know who's behind the mask. I've found my ideal partner for this kind of concept, so that I can stay behind the scenes, as artistic director, while showcasing youth! The comfort I have in TGDD is that Joy runs everything. I only do the sketches. It's my ideal situation, it's the ideal situation for an aging creative who no longer has any patience with clients, craftworkers, or anything else. He just wants to draw! As long as my hand doesn't shake! Even if it did, maybe it could be an interesting tool!"

EXTRACT OF TGDD COMICS, WHERE JOY AND GREGORY ARE SITTING IN THE LOTUS POSITION NEXT TO EACH OTHER IN A SNOW-COVERED FIELD SURROUNDED BY SNOW-COVERED PEAKS—THE ALPS, PERHAPS, OR THE HIMALAYAS EVEN, 2019

Biography

Of Georgian roots (1951), Gregory Gatserelia was raised and educated in France. After school, he joined his family in Lebanon, his mother's home country, where he decided to follow his passion for art and design at his beloved Académie Libanaise des Beaux-Arts, earning a degree in interior design.

In 1987, Gregory made one of his most defining moves by opening Gatserelia Design International in Toronto, Canada, with his brother Alexandre. When the horrifying civil war in Lebanon ended, Gatserelia saw a remarkable opportunity to contribute to the nation's reconstruction while being a part of a remarkably vital creative scene. In 1996, he moved the company's central office to the jewel-city of Beirut. From there, Gregory quickly moved across the globe, leaving his signature on an immense array of projects, whose shared qualities included innovation, functionality, beauty, and sustainability. Since then, his success and growth have been continuous, together with praise for his work internationally. *Architectural Digest* listed him as one of the world's top interior designers on more than one occasion. However, the drive behind Gregory's work is bound up with his ceaseless creative impulse, informed by everything from literature to film to his most personal experiences and emotions and, of course, the one constant: his profound love of art and design itself.

Gregory also actively continues his work as an art curator, as he did in the past by opening the SMO Gallery in Beirut in 2011, promoting up-and-coming talents who subsequently went on to enjoy major success.

Since 1985 and to the present, Gatserelia Design has brought his unwavering creative integrity to architectural projects in both the private and public sectors. His work includes construction of high-end residential projects and corporate offices, as well as international award-winning designs for the hospitality and food-service industries. In 2019, he has begun a truly unique project in the great design city of Milan with Joy Herro. This is The Great Design Disaster, a start-up devoted to facilitating collectors in bringing their own creativity to the works they acquire by walking them through the whole creative process with handpicked artisans.

Photographers' Credits and Design List

COVER
© Francis Amiand
Art & Design: *Naturoscopie II* chandelier, Noé Duchaufour-Lawrance, 2013; SMO Gallery, *Wave* dining table, Georges Mohasseb, 2013; Knoll, *Model no. 71* dining chairs, Eero Saarinen, 1960s; *Lacrime di Coccodrillo* candlestick, Campana Brothers, 2012 © Fernando Piva Campana by SIAE 2023.

PHOTOS OF BEIRUT
© Ieva Saudargaitė
pp. 22–23, 26, 27, 28, 31, 32, 33, 34–35

pp. 10, 140: © Joe Kesrouani. **Art & Design:** *How High the Moon* armchair, Shirō Kuramata, SMO Gallery Beirut (Lebanon), 2011
p. 12: © Charbel Saade. **Art & Design:** long night chair, Wendell Castle, 2011; *Osselet* side table, Jean-Marc Lelouch, 2015; pair of armchairs, Gio Ponti, 1950s; *Patte d'Ours* ashtray table, Georges Jouve & Mathieu Matégot, 1951 by SIAE 2023; *La Fente*, sculpture, Philippe Hiquily, 1993 by SIAE 2023; curved sofa, Ico Parisi, 1958; coffee table, Ado Chale, 1985 by SIAE 2023
p. 14: © Charbel Saadeh
pp. 16–21, 24, 25, 81, 227:
© Archive Gregory Gatserelia
p. 29: © Leo Fabrizi
p. 30: © Roads for Life Charity

RESIDENTIAL INTERIORS

Downtown, Beirut (Lebanon), 2013
pp. 38, 42–63: © Francis Amiand
p. 41: © Eva Szumilas

Art & Design
p. 38: *R12* side table, Thierry Lemaire, 2013; SMO Gallery, *Talon Aiguille* coffee table, Georges Mohasseb, 2013; *Torero*, sculpture, Miguel Berrocal, 1970s by SIAE 2023; *More is More* bench, Wendell Castle, 2011; The Rug Company, *Pale Swirl* carpet, Paul Smith, 2000.
p. 41: Sursock, Beirut (Lebanon), 2009: *Timeline*, sculpture, Tony Cragg, 2008 by SIAE 2023; *Copper Surrogate* panels, Walead Beshty, 2011.
pp. 42–43: coffee table, Armand Jonckers, 1970s by SIAE 2023; sculpture, Parvine Curie, 1970s by SIAE 2023; sculpture, Monique Rozanès, 2000s by SIAE 2023; The Rug Company, *Silhouette* carpet, Jaime Hayon, 2011; *X-Stool* stool, Michel Boyer,

1968; *Stoneware* side table, GamFratesi, 2012; Poltrona Frau, *Archibald* armchairs, Jean-Marie Massaud, 2009; Poltrona Frau, *Willy* armchairs, Guglielmo Ulrich, 2012; sculpture, Claude Mercier, c. 1987 by SIAE 2023; obelisks, Jean-Claude Farhi, 2000s by SIAE 2023; video loop *Mademoiselle Caroline Rivière d'après Jean-Auguste-Dominique Ingres*, Robert Wilson, 2013; *Rhinocéros Bleu*, sculpture, François-Xavier Lalanne, 1980s by SIAE 2023; *Pair*, sculpture, Tony Cragg, 2012 by SIAE 2023.
p. 44: Cassina, *Utrecht* armchairs, Gerrit Thomas Rietveld, 1988 by SIAE 2023; The Rug Company, *Stripe* carpet, Paul Smith, 2000; cabinet, Pierre Cardin, 1980s; Artemide, *Cosmic Angel* chandelier, Ross Lovegrove, 2009; *Scramble* floor lamp, Mauro Fabbro, 2009.
p. 45: pair of totems, Jean-Claude Farhi, 2000s by SIAE 2023; The Rug Company, *Stripe* carpet, Paul Smith, 2000; *Scramble* floor lamp, Mauro Fabbro, 2009.
pp. 46–47: *Pierre's Sheep*, sculpture, François-Xavier Lalanne, c. 1986 by SIAE 2023; *Champignons* side tables, Philippe Hiquily, c. 1975 by SIAE 2023; Knoll, *Platner Easy Chair* armchairs, Warren Platner, 1966; *Round* sofa, Gregory Gatserelia, 2009; Manifattura Ceramica Bitossi, *Odalisca* totem, Ettore Sottsass, 1988 by SIAE 2023; *Mère Cathédrale*, sculpture, Parvine Curie, 1997 by SIAE 2023; *Catch* chandelier, Lindsey Adelman, 2013.
p. 48: cabinet, Paul Evans, 1970s.
p. 49: mirrored hallway with bronze sconces, Gregory Gatserelia, 2013.
p. 50: *Pair*, sculpture, Tony Cragg, 2012 by SIAE 2023; *X-Stool* stool, Michel Boyer, 1968; *X-Table* side table, Michel Boyer, 1968; coffee table, Jacques Duval Brasseur, 1970s by SIAE 2023.
p. 51: sculpture, Dietrich-Mohr, 1980s by SIAE 2023; *Bornes*, sculpture, Jean-Claude Farhi, 1970 by SIAE 2023.
pp. 52–53: *Stoneware* side table, GamFratesi, 2012; Poltrona Frau, *Archibald* armchairs, Jean-Marie Massaud, 2009; The Rug Company, *Silhouette* carpet, Jaime Hayon, 2011; coffee table, Armand Jonckers, 1970 by SIAE 2023; sculpture, Parvine Curie, 1970s by SIAE 2023; sculpture, Monique Rozanès, 2000s by SIAE 2023; sculpture, Claude Mercier, c. 1987 by SIAE 2023; Poltrona Frau, *Willy* armchairs, Guglielmo Ulrich, 2012; *Anneaux* table, Ingrid Donat, 2008; *Scholar Rocks* table lamp, Peter Lane and Chahan Minassian, 2013; *Lampada White Gold* lamp, Alessandro Mendini, 2002; *Pierre's Sheep*, sculpture, François-Xavier Lalanne, c. 1986 by SIAE 2023; *Champignons* side tables, Philippe Hiquily, c. 1975 by SIAE 2023; Knoll, *Platner Easy Chair* armchairs, Warren Platner, 1966; *Odalisca* totem, Ettore Sottsass, 1988 by SIAE 2023; *Round* sofa, Gregory Gatserelia, 2009; *Mère Cathédrale*, sculpture, Parvine Curie, 1997 by SIAE 2023; *Catch* chandelier, Lindsey Adelman, 2013.
p. 54: bookshelf, Gregory Gatserelia, 2013.
p. 55: *Hiroshima II* table lamp, Karen Chekerdjian, 2013; *Prehistoric Bird* wall light, Félix Agostini, 1960 by SIAE 2023.
pp. 56–57: SMO Gallery Beirut, double-sided sofa, Gregory Gatserelia, 2013; *Six Stools* stools, Karen Chekerdjian, 2009; totem, César Baldaccini and Jean-Claude Farhi, 1960s by SIAE 2023; panels, Atelier Zimmermann, 2013; cabinet, Paul Evans, 1970s; *Standing/Sitting* bar, Gregory Gatserelia, 2013; Philippe Hiquily, 1960 by SIAE 2023; *Menta* totem, Ettore Sottsass, 1985 by SIAE 2023.
pp. 58–59: *Naturoscopie II* chandelier, Noé Duchaufour-Lawrance, 2013; SMO Gallery, *Wave* dining table, Georges Mohasseb, 2013; Knoll, *Model no. 71* dining chairs, Eero Saarinen, 1960s; *Lacrime di Coccodrillo* candlestick, Campana Brothers, 2012 by SIAE 2023; totem, Martino Gamper, 2007; panels, Atelier Zimmermann, 2013; sculpture, Dietrich-Mohr, 1980s by SIAE 2023; *Bornes* totem, Jean-Claude Farhi, 1970 by SIAE 2023.
p. 60: *Grisaille*, photograph by Marie Bovo, 2010.
p. 61: SMO Gallery Beirut, double-sided sofa, Gregory Gatserelia, 2013; *Six Stools* stools, Karen Chekerdjian, 2009; totem, César Baldaccini and Jean-Claude Farhi, 1960s by SIAE 2023; panels, Atelier Zimmermann, 2013; *Untitled*, charcoal, Robert Longo, 2010s by SIAE 2023.
pp. 62–63: SMO Gallery Beirut, *Edna* swing chair, Karim Chaaya, 2013; *Holey Nite* side table, Wendell Castle, 2011; coffee table, Jacques Duval Brasseur, 1970s by SIAE 2023; *X-Stool* stool, Michel Boyer, 1968.

Achrafieh, Beirut (Lebanon), 2019
pp. 64–73: © Eva Szumilas

Art & Design
pp. 64–65: Cassina, *Doge* dining table, Carlo Scarpa, 1968; Maxalto, *Artona* dining chairs, Afra and Tobia Scarpa, 1975; *12 arms* chandelier, Hans Agne Jakobsson, 1960; Singer & Sons, cabinet, Gio Ponti, 1950; *Mod. 206* wall lights, Gino Sarfatti,

1950; *Santa Cruz* tapestry, Mathieu Matégot, 1950 by SIAE 2023; sculpture, Émile Gilioli, 1950s by SIAE 2023; desk and chair, Jean Albert Théophile Royère, 1950s by SIAE 2023.
p. 66: *Le Centaure*, sculpture, Claude and François-Xavier Lalanne, c. 1988 by SIAE 2023.
p. 67: Cassina, *Doge* dining table, Carlo Scarpa, 1968; Maxalto, *Artona* dining chairs, Afra and Tobia Scarpa, 1975; *12 arms* chandelier, Hans Agne Jakobsson, 1960; Singer & Sons, cabinet, Gio Ponti, 1950; *Mod. 206* wall lights, Gino Sarfatti, 1950; *Santa Cruz* tapestry, Mathieu Matégot, 1950 by SIAE 2023.
pp. 68–69: armchairs, Gio Ponti, 1950; coffee table, Alain Delon, 1970; *Cité* daybed, Jean Prouvé, 1950; FontanaArte, ashtray table, Max Ingrand, 1960 by SIAE 2023; *Joliejoie* barstools, The Great Design Disaster, 2019; bar ceramics artistic cladding, Hala Matta, 2019.
p. 70: *Cité* daybed, Jean Prouvé, 1950; FontanaArte, ashtray table, Max Ingrand, 1960 by SIAE 2023; armchairs, Gio Ponti, 1950; floor lamp, Pierre Guariche, 1950s; coffee table, Alain Delon, 1970; *Isa* sofa, 1950s; Arredoluce, *Eye* floor lamp, Angelo Lelli, c. 1955.
p. 71: FontanaArte, *Dahlia* wall light, Max Ingrand, 1955 by SIAE 2023.
p. 72: *Multistrata* side table, Gregory Gatserelia, 2013; *Rare Lune* light sculpture, Gabriella Crespi, 1970; *Plurimi* coffee table, Gabriella Crespi, 1970s; stools, Marie-Claude de Fouquières, 1970s by SIAE 2023; *Tube et Béret* floor lamp, Andrée Putman, 2003 by SIAE 2023; *Cubi* side table, Francesco Santo Chirico, 2018; sculpture, Émile Gilioli, 1950s by SIAE 2023.
p. 73: sculpture, Émile Gilioli, 1950s by SIAE 2023; desk, Jean Albert Théophile Royère, 1950s by SIAE 2023.

Downtown, Beirut (Lebanon), 2018
pp. 74–80: © Eva Szumilas

Art & Design
pp. 74–75: SMO Gallery, round sofa, Gregory Gatserelia, 2009; set of *Joséphine* coffee tables, Ado Chale, 2013 by SIAE 2023; *Monsieur et Madame* side tables, Philippe Hiquily, 1977 by SIAE 2023; pair of lounge chairs, Percival Lafer, 1972; carpet, Iwan Maktabi, 2009; *Riflessione* floor lamp, Claudio Salocchi, 1973; *L'Homme à La Roue*, sculpture, Armin Göhringer, 1980.
pp. 76–77: *Puerta de La Luna* console, Monique Rozanès, 1980 by SIAE 2023; *Courtrai* daybed, Bruno Moinard Éditions, 2014; *Tari* coffee tables, Bruno Moinard Éditions, 2014; carpet, Iwan Maktabi, 2009; *Osselet* side table, Jean-Marc Lelouch, 2010; *L'Homme à La Roue*, sculpture, Armin Göhringer, 1980.
pp. 78–79: *Totem* lighting fixtures, Bethan Laura Wood, 2011; set of dining table, sideboard, mirror *Party,* Gregory Gatserelia, 2018; Giorgetti, *Ode* dining chairs, Chi Wing Lo, 2012; *Nénuphar* floor lamp, Philippe Hiquily, 1985 by SIAE 2023.
p. 80: *Totem* lighting fixtures, Bethan Laura Wood, 2011.

Wadi Abou Jamil, Beirut (Lebanon), 2018
pp. 82–91: © Eva Szumilas

Art & Design
p. 82: sculptural staircase, Gregory Gatserelia, 2018; Knoll, *Tulip* dining table and chairs, Eero Saarinen, 1957.
p. 83: dining table and sideboard, Valentin Loellmann, 2018; Thonet, *S64* chairs, Marcel Breuer, 1930s; site-specific raku wall sculpture, Marylynn Massoud and Rasha Nawam, 2018; set of three *Sajla* kinetic chandeliers, Gregory Gatserelia, 2018.
pp. 84–85: *24 squares superimposed on 3* kinetic sculpture table, Pol Bury, 1990 by SIAE 2023; Maxalto, set of *Artona* coffee tables, Afra and Tobia Scarpa, 1975; pair of *Sci-Fi* vases, Marc Newson, 1993; FontanaArte, glass objects, Max Ingrand, 1960s by SIAE 2023; ceramics, Frères Cloutiers, 1960; *Mobile*, sculpture, François Colette, 1970s; side table, Philippe Hiquily, 1960s by SIAE 2023; pair of *055 Capitol Complex* chairs, Pierre Jeanneret, 1950s by SIAE 2023; Morphos Acerbis Editions, Lella and Massimo Vignelli, 1980s; carpet, Iwan Maktabi, 2018; artwork, Victor Vasarely, c. 1955 by SIAE 2023.
p. 86: *Edmond De Rothschild* coffee table, Philippe Hiquily, 1965 by SIAE 2023; *Meteor* coffee table, Arik Levy, 2005; Iwan Maktabi, *Scene 1 - Odyssey Collection* carpet, Gregory Gatserelia, 2018; pair of *Scholar Rocks* table lamps, Peter Lane and Chahan Minassian, 2013; *Caracalla* vase, Martine Bedin, 2006 by SIAE 2023; *Untitled (City)*, painting, Tobias Pils, 2016; *Untitled (Autumn 1)*, painting, Tobias Pils, 2015.
p. 87: *Volcanique* console, Ado Chale, 1980 by SIAE 2023; *Retour du Guerrier*, sculpture, Benito Viliano Tarabella, 1962; decorative wall, Hervouet, 2018.

pp. 88–89: pair of *RCU* armchairs, Niko Koronis, 2016; pair of *Scholar Rocks* table lamps, Peter Lane and Chahan Minassian, 2013; *Edmond De Rothschild* coffee table, Philippe Hiquily, 1965 by SIAE 2023; Iwan Maktabi, *Scene 1 - Odyssey Collection* carpet, Gregory Gatserelia, 2018; *Untitled (City)*, painting, Tobias Pils, 2016; *Untitled (Autumn 1)*, painting, Tobias Pils, 2015; *Meteor* coffee table, Arik Levy, 2005; *Helicoid* staircase sculpture, Roger Tallon, 1960; *Osselet* side table, Jean-Marc Lelouch, 2016; lounge chair, George Nakashima, 1965; side table, Gabriella Crespi, 1970s.
p. 90: Maxalto, set of *Artona* coffee tables, Afra and Tobia Scarpa, 1975; *Mobile*, sculpture, François Colette, 1970s; pair of *055 Capitol Complex* chairs, Pierre Jeanneret, 1950s by SIAE 2023; carpet, Iwan Maktabi, 2018; *Untitled (Shere Khan)*, painting, Robert Longo, 2016 by SIAE 2023.
p. 91: *Helicoid* staircase sculpture, Roger Tallon, 1960; *Osselet* side table, Jean-Marc Lelouch, 2016; *Meteor* coffee table, Arik Levy, 2005; pair of *Scholar Rocks* table lamps, Peter Lane and Chahan Minassian, 2013; *Untitled (City)*, painting, Tobias Pils, 2016; *Untitled (Autumn 1)*, painting, Tobias Pils, 2015.

Twin Towers, Achrafieh, Beirut (Lebanon), 2010
pp. 92–97: © Elie Bakhazi

Art & Design
p. 92: cement red tunnel, Gregory Gatserelia, 2010; *Volcanique* console, Ado Chale, 1980; mirror, Jacques Duval Brasseur, 1970s; totem, Ettore Sottsass, c. 1967.
p. 93: armchair, Walter & Moretti, 1970; floor lamp, Philippe Jean, 1970; De Sede, *Non Stop* sofa, Heinz Ulrich, Eleonora Peduzzi Riva, Ueli Berger, 1980s; panels, Atelier Zimmermann, 2010.
pp. 94–95: De Sede, *Non Stop* sofa, Heinz Ulrich, Eleonora Peduzzi Riva, Ueli Berger, 1980s; cement red tunnel, Gregory Gatserelia, 2010; *Volcanique* console, Ado Chale, 1980 by SIAE 2023; mirror, Jacques Duval Brasseur, 1970s by SIAE 2023; totem, Ettore Sottsass, c. 1967 by SIAE 2023; *Leda* coffee table, Philippe Hiquily, 2005 by SIAE 2023; *Parmigianino Sphere 24*, Martin C. Herbst, 2017; *Embryo* chair, Marc Newson, 1988 painting, Ayman Baalbaki, 2010.
pp. 96–97: dining table, Gregory Gatserelia, 2010; *Robert Hass* dining chairs, Philippe Hiquily, 1967 by SIAE 2023; *Confusion* suspension, Hervé van der Straeten, 2008; panels, Atelier Zimmermann, 2010.

Manara, Beirut (Lebanon), 2015
pp. 98–105: © Charbel Saade

Art & Design
pp. 98–99: *DC1204* bench, Vincenzo De Cotiis, 2012; set of *Joséphine* coffee tables, Ado Chale, 2013 by SIAE 2023; *Colonne Organique* totem, François Kovacs, 1972; *Champignons* side tables, Philippe Hiquily, c. 1975 by SIAE 2023; coffee table, Ado Chale, 1985 by SIAE 2023; long night chair, Wendell Castle, 2011; *Soucoupe Grand Modèle* floor lamp, Yonel Lebovici, 1978 by SIAE 2023; curved sofa, Ico Parisi, 1958; *Osselet* side table, Jean-Marc Lelouch, 2015; coffee table, Ado Chale, 1985 by SIAE 2023.
p. 100: bar, Gregory Gatserelia, 2015; candleholder, Gregory Gatserelia, 2015.
p. 101: *Bell* side tables, Sebastian Herkner, 2012; pair of armchairs, Marco Zanuso, 1950; coffee table, Gerard Kuijpers, 2013; *Soucoupe Grand Modèle* floor lamp, Yonel Lebovici, 1978 by SIAE 2023; curved sofa, Ico Parisi, 1958; *Osselet* side table, Jean-Marc Lelouch, 2015.
pp. 102–103: *DC1204* bench, Vincenzo De Cotiis, 2012; set of *Joséphine* coffee tables, Ado Chale, 2013 by SIAE 2023; *Colonne Organique* totem, François Kovacs, 1972; *Champignons* side tables, Philippe Hiquily, c. 1975 by SIAE 2023.
pp. 104–105: *Tube et Béret* floor lamp, Andrée Putman, 2003 by SIAE 2023; coffee table, Gerard Kuijpers, 2013; *Bell* side tables, Sebastian Herkner, 2012; pair of armchairs, Marco Zanuso, 1950; bar, Gregory Gatserelia, 2015; *Colonne Organique* totem, François Kovacs, 1972; *DC1204* bench, Vincenzo De Cotiis, 2012; set of *Joséphine* coffee tables, Ado Chale, 2013 by SIAE 2023; *Colonne Organique* totem, François Kovacs, 1972; *Champignons* side tables, Philippe Hiquily, c. 1975 by SIAE 2023; long night chair, Wendell Castle, 2011; *Soucoupe Grand Modèle* floor lamp, Yonel Lebovici, 1978 by SIAE 2023.

Platinum Tower, Zaitunay, Beirut (Lebanon), 2016
pp. 106–119: © Francis Amiand

Art & Design
p. 106: armchair, Marco Zanuso, 1950s; *Copeaux* table, Ado Chale, 1970 by SIAE 2023; *Relief d'Agate* table, Ado Chale, 1975 by SIAE 2023; *Ostsee am Strand*, painting, Georg Baselitz, 2011; carpet, Bruno Moinard, 2010.
p. 107: *Anneaux* coffee table, Ingrid Donat, 2013; *Wave*, painting, Takesada Matsutani, 1987; *DC1204* bench, Vincenzo De Cotiis, 2012; *Timeline*,

sculpture, Tony Cragg, 2008 by SIAE 2023; *Lutteurs*, sculpture, Jacques Charles Zwobada, 1954 by SIAE 2023.
pp. 108–109: *Brutalist* dining table, Paul Evans, 1974; *Flylight* chandelier, Studio Drift, 2011; sideboard, Gregory Gatserelia, 2016; *Astrale*, sculpture, Émile Gilioli, 1966 by SIAE 2023; curved panels, Gregory Gatserelia, 2016; armchair, Marco Zanuso, 1950s; *Copeaux* table, Ado Chale, 1970 by SIAE 2023; *Relief d'Agate* table, Ado Chale, 1975 by SIAE 2023; *Ostsee am Strand*, painting, Georg Baselitz, 2011.
p. 110: *Multistrata* table, Gregory Gatserelia, 2013; sideboard, Gregory Gatserelia, 2016; *Vaires*, painting, Georges Mathieu, 1965 by SIAE 2023.
p. 111: Fiam, coffee table, Danny Lane, 1980s; coffee table *Basoli*, Campana Brothers, 2011 © Fernando Piva Campana by SIAE 2023; *Old Hollywood Movies*, nine photographs by Jack Pierson, 2010; *Eagle Royal*, painting, Yan Pei-Ming, 2013 by SIAE 2023; *Happiness* armchair, Damien Langlois-Meurinne, 2007; side table, Vincenzo De Cotiis, 2013; *Scholar Rock* table lamp, Peter Lane & Chahan Minassian, 2013; carpet, Iwan Maktabi, 2016.
pp. 112–113: armchair, Marco Zanuso, 1950s; side table, Oeuffice, 2011; *Copeaux* table, Ado Chale, 1970 by SIAE 2023; *Relief d'Agate* table, Ado Chale, 1975 by SIAE 2023; *Ostsee am Strand*, painting, Georg Baselitz, 2011; *Serpentine* sofa and pouf, Vladimir Kagan, 1950s; carpet, Bruno Moinard, 2010.
p. 114: wall lights, Armand Jonckers, 1970s by SIAE 2023.
p. 115: pair of armchairs, Jacques Adnet, 1950s by SIAE 2023; side table, Oeuffice, 2011.
pp. 116–117: *DC1204* bench, Vincenzo De Cotiis, 2012; *Timeline*, sculpture, Tony Cragg, 2008 by SIAE 2023; *Quilles Décentrées* side tables, Philippe Hiquily, 1970 by SIAE 2023; *Anneaux* coffee table, Ingrid Donat, 2013; *Lutteurs*, sculpture, Jacques Charles Zwobada, 1954 by SIAE 2023; pair of *Multistrata* tables, Gregory Gatserelia, 2013; sideboard, Gregory Gatserelia, 2016; *Vaires*, painting, Georges Mathieu, 1965 by SIAE 2023; *Astrale*, sculpture, Émile Gilioli, 1966 by SIAE 2023; curved panels, Gregory Gatserelia, 2016; cabinet, Paul Evans, 1970s; UP Závody, pair of *H269* armchairs, Jindrich Halabala, 1930s; *Galileo*, painting, Jason Martin, 2013 by SIAE 2023.
p. 118: *DC1204* bench, Vincenzo De Cotiis, 2012; *Timeline*, sculpture, Tony Cragg, 2008 by SIAE 2023; *All in All*, sculpture, Tony Cragg, 2013 by SIAE 2023; sideboard, Gregory Gatserelia, 2016.
p. 119: handle, Gregory Gatserelia, 2016.

Sursock, Beirut (Lebanon), 2013
pp. 120–125: ©Vicky Mokbel

Art & Design
p. 120: *Pompei* chairs, Alberto Orlandi, 1980s; coffee table, Fred Brouard, c. 1974 by SIAE 2023.
p. 121: *Meteor* coffee tables, Arik Levy, 2005; *Falcon* armchair, Sigurd Russell, 1970; *Serpentine* sofa, Vladimir Kagan, 1950s; Vibia, *Samurai* floor lamp, Robby Cantarutti, 2011.
pp. 122–123: dining table, Gregory Gatserelia, 2013; *Fragile Future* chandelier, Studio Drift, 2007; ceramics, Nathalie Khayat, 2013; panels, Atelier Zimmermann, 2013; *Blossom* ceramic, Wieki Somers, 2005; *Simon* candleholder, Bořek Šipek, 1980s; sculpture, Mozart Guerra, 2013 by SIAE 2023.
p. 124: *Souffle du Desert* cabinet, Vincent Dubourg, 2008 by SIAE 2023; *Burka*, charcoal, Robert Longo, 2010 by SIAE 2023.
p. 125: mirror, Gregory Gatserelia, 2013.

Sursock, Beirut (Lebanon), 2009
pp. 126–139: © Eva Szumilas

Art & Design
pp. 126–127: sculpture, Tony Cragg, by SIAE 2023; private commission, dining table and chandelier, Ross Lovegrove, 2009; *Untitled (Tiger)*, charcoal, Robert Longo, by SIAE 2023.
p. 128: private commission, dining table and chandelier, Ross Lovegrove, 2009; *Untitled (Tiger)*, charcoal, Robert Longo, by SIAE 2023; wall sculpture, Armen Agop Guerboyan, 2010 by SIAE 2023; Artemide, *Lavinia* table lamps, Masayuki Kurosawa, 1988.
p. 129: *Ahnenstunde*, oil on canvas, Georg Baselitz, 2012; *Wood Ring* bench, Chris Kabel, 2011.
pp. 130–131: *Ahnenstunde*, oil on canvas, Georg Baselitz, 2012; *Wood Ring* bench, Chris Kabel, 2011; *Copper Surrogate* panels, Walead Beshty, 2011.
p. 132: *Frog* table, Hella Jongerius, 2009.
p. 133: *Wood Ring* bench, Chris Kabel, 2011; *Copper Surrogate* panels, Walead Beshty, 2011; *Untitled (Tiger)*, charcoal, Robert Longo, by SIAE 2023; *Sunset (White)* lightbox, Doug Aitken, 2011; *Falcon* armchairs, Sigmund Russel, 1970; *Super Guppy* floor lamp, Marc Newson, 1987.
p. 134: *Baalbeck*, photograph by Ziad Antar, 2016; *Duplex* stool, Javier Mariscal, 1980s by SIAE 2023;

Cassina, *K10 Dodo* lounge chair, Toshiyuki Kita, 2000.
p. 135: *Metal Box* wall sculpture, Jim Lambie, by SIAE 2023; *Afterimage 08-297* side table, Choï Byung Hoon, 2008.
pp. 136–137: *Sunset (White)* lightbox, Doug Aitken, 2011; *Falcon* armchairs, Sigmund Russel, 1970; *Serpentine* sofa, Vladimir Kagan, 1950s; *Super Guppy* floor lamp, Marc Newson, 1987; coffee table, Ado Chale, 1980s by SIAE 2023; side table, Karen Chekerdjian, 2006.

Ain El Mreysseh, Beirut (Lebanon), 2023
pp. 141–155: © Eva Szumilas

Art & Design
p. 141: Molteni & C., *D.153.1* armchair, Gio Ponti, 2012; *DC1717* coffee table, Vincenzo De Cotiis, 2017; Galerie Kreo, *Perugia* coffee table, Alessandro Mendini, 2001; *Bright Cell*, sculpture, Hitomi Uchikura, 2021; FontanaArte, *Mod. 1977* serre livre, Max Ingrand, 1960s by SIAE 2023; sculpture, François Kovacs, 1965; ashtray, Paolo De Poli, 1960s; The Great Design Disaster, *Cedrus Imprints* side table, Gregory Gatserelia & Alessandro Rametta, 2020; pair of *Pegasi* sculptural lamps, Emmanuel Jonckers, 2019; *Cityscape* sofa, Paul Evans, 1960s.
pp. 142–143: cabinet of curiosity, Gregory Gatserelia, 2020; *Blossom* vases, Studio Wieki Somers, 2004; *Carpe d'Or*, sculpture, François-Xavier Lalanne, 1987 by SIAE 2023; *Architectural Glass Fantasies no. 44*, sculpture, Stine Bidstrup, 2019; *Architectural Glass Fantasies no. 46*, sculpture, Stine Bidstrup, 2019; *Crystallization 166*, sculpture, Lukas Wegwerth, 2021; *Crystallization 168*, sculpture, Lukas Wegwerth, 2021; sculpture, Harumi Nakashima, 2016; *Pair*, sculpture, Tony Cragg, 2019 by SIAE 2023; *Joliejoie* dining table, Gregory Gatserelia, 2019; The Great Design Disaster, *Fan* chandeliers, Gregory Gatserelia, 2020; *Red Sky Mirror*, sculpture, Anish Kapoor, 2016. All Rights Reserved, DACS/SIAE; sideboard and handles, Gregory Gatserelia, 2019; Dom Pérignon, *Balloon Venus*, sculpture, Jeff Koons, 2003; *Scale to Infinity - Fragment 8*, sculpture, Audrey Large, 2021; *Bright Cell*, sculpture, Hitomi Uchikura, 2021; pair of candleholders, Victor Roman, 1970 by SIAE 2023; *Le Samurai*, sculpture, Franco Adami, 1980s by SIAE 2023; *Solune* coffee table, Ado Chale, 2010s by SIAE 2023; *Paire de Quilles* side table, Philippe Hiquily, 1960s by SIAE 2023; The Great Design Disaster, pair of *Race* armchairs, Gregory Gatserelia, 2020; *Goosefish* lamp, Carlo Lorenzetti, 2020; *Ruche* lamp, Michel Armand, 1970s.
p. 144: sofa, Federico Munari, 1955; pair of *Matacubo* sculptures, Pietro Consagra, 1997 by SIAE 2023; *Imaginary Crystallisations no. 1*, sculpture, Stine Bidstrup, 2019; The Great Design Disaster, *Playtime* coffee table, Gregory Gatserelia, 2020; pair of *7A/8 – 7B/8* sculptures, Jean-Claude Farhi & César Baldaccini, 1960s by SIAE 2023.
p. 145: *Solune* coffee table, Ado Chale, 2010s by SIAE 2023; *Bright Cell*, sculpture, Hitomi Uchikura, 2021; *Il Diavolo* mask, Gio Ponti, 1970s; pair of candleholders, Victor Roman, 1970 by SIAE 2023; *Scale to Infinity - Fragment 8*, sculpture, Audrey Large, 2021; *Le Samurai*, sculpture, Franco Adami, 1980s by SIAE 2023; *Architectural Glass Fantasies no. 55*, sculpture, Stine Bidstrup, 2021; *Veilleuse*, sculpture, Robert Goossens, 1980s by SIAE 2023; ashtray, Georges Jouve, 1955; *Mini Maria*, sculpture, Miguel Berrocal, c. 1968 by SIAE 2023; *Artbook Chevet* side table, Ingrid Donat, 2011; *Ruche* lamp, Michel Armand, 1970s; The Great Design Disaster, *Tetris* side table, Gregory Gatserelia, 2020; The Great Design Disaster, pair of *Race* armchairs, Gregory Gatserelia, 2020; sculpture, Harumi Nakashima, 2016; *Paire de Quilles* side table, Philippe Hiquily, 1960s by SIAE 2023; cabinet of curiosity, Gregory Gatserelia, 2020; sculpture, Ernst Scheubeck, 1970s; *Partitions Azules* totem, Monique Rozanès, 2014 by SIAE 2023; *Blossom* vases, Studio Wieki Somers, 2004; pair of sculptures, Chieko Katsumata, 2021; *Pyramide Cubiste*, sculpture, Monique Rozanès, 2014 by SIAE 2023; *Architectural Glass Fantasies no. 44*, sculpture, Stine Bidstrup, 2019; *Architectural Glass Fantasies no. 46*, sculpture, Stine Bidstrup, 2019; *Carpe d'Or*, sculpture, François-Xavier Lalanne, 1987 by SIAE 2023; *Crystallization 166*, sculpture, Lukas Wegwerth, 2021; *Crystallization 168*, sculpture, Lukas Wegwerth, 2021; sculpture, Viliano Tarabella, 1970s; sculpture, Philolaos Tloupas, 1970s by SIAE 2023; *Mecca*, charcoal on mounted paper, Robert Longo, 2020 by SIAE 2023.
pp. 146–147: *Solune* coffee table, Ado Chale, 2010s by SIAE 2023; *Bright Cell*, sculpture, Hitomi Uchikura, 2021; *Il Diavolo* mask, Gio Ponti, 1970s; pair of candleholders, Victor Roman, 1970 by SIAE 2023; *Scale to Infinity - Fragment 8*, sculpture, Audrey Large, 2021; *Architectural Glass Fantasies no. 55*, sculpture, Stine Bidstrup, 2021; *Veilleuse*, sculpture, Robert Goossens, 1980s

by SIAE 2023; ashtray, Georges Jouve, 1955; *Mini Maria*, sculpture, Miguel Berrocal, c. 1968 by SIAE 2023; *Scale to Infinity - Fragment 8*, sculpture, Audrey Large, 2021; *Le Samurai*, sculpture, Franco Adami, 1980s by SIAE 2023; The Great Design Disaster, *Race* armchair, Gregory Gatserelia, 2020; *Artbook Chevet* side table, Ingrid Donat, 2011; *Goosefish* lamp, Carlo Lorenzetti, 2020; *Paire de Quilles* side table, Philippe Hiquily, 1960s by SIAE 2023; *Stack*, sculpture, Annie Morris, 2021; The Great Design Disaster, *Fan* chandeliers, Gregory Gatserelia, 2020; sideboard and handles, Gregory Gatserelia, 2019; The Great Design Disaster, *Tetris* side table, Gregory Gatserelia, 2020; *Sweet Tiger*, charcoal, Robert Longo, 2021 by SIAE 2023; The Great Design Disaster, console, Gregory Gatserelia, 2020; *Crystallization 170*, sculpture, Lukas Wegwerth, 2021.
p. 148: *Love Difference* mirror, Michelangelo Pistoletto, 2002; *Balloon Swan Magenta*, sculpture, Jeff Koons, 2019; *Balloon Swan Yellow*, sculpture, Jeff Koons, 2019; *Balloon Rabbit Blue*, sculpture, Jeff Koons, 2019; *Balloon Rabbit Orange*, sculpture, Jeff Koons, 2019; TV cabinet, Gregory Gatserelia, 2020; sculpture, Fred Brouard, 1970s by SIAE 2023; bowl, Ado Chale, 1970s by SIAE 2023; coffee table, Ateliers Oeufs, 1970s; *Transparence Mystique* totem, Monique Rozanès, c. 2006s by SIAE 2023.
p. 149: *Collier Autoporté*, sculpture, Jean-Michel Othoniel, 2020 by SIAE 2023; *Transparence Mystique* totem, Monique Rozanès, c. 2006 by SIAE 2023.
p. 150: *Cyclade* cabinet, François Cante, 1970s by SIAE 2023; Flos, *Taccia* table lamp, Achille and Pier Giacomo Castiglioni, 1962.
p. 151: *Red Sky Mirror*, sculpture, Anish Kapoor, 2016. All Rights Reserved, DACS/SIAE; sideboard and handles, Gregory Gatserelia, 2019; Dom Pérignon, *Balloon Venus*, sculpture, Jeff Koons, 2003.
p. 152: photograph by Anwar Azzi, 2020; *Agra* totem, Ettore Sottsass, c. 1994 by SIAE 2023.
p. 153: sculpture, Jean-Claude Farhi, 2006s by SIAE 2023; *Cubi* side table, Francesco Santo Chirico, 2020; Flos, *Snoopy* table lamp, Achille and Pier Giacomo Castiglioni, 1967.
p. 154: The Great Design Disaster, pair of *Lamppost* night stands, Gregory Gatserelia, 2020; The Great Design Disaster, bed, Gregory Gatserelia, 2020; The Great Design Disaster, bench, Gregory Gatserelia, 2020; The Great Design Disaster, *Space* chandelier, Gregory Gatserelia, 2020.
p. 155: *Sun*, painting, Ugo Rondinone, 2022.

14 Rue François 1er, Paris (France), 2023
pp. 156–159: © Gaëlle Le Boulicaut

Art & Design
p. 156: *Terra Incognita* coffee table, Béatrice Serre, 2022 by SIAE 2023; *Pigeon* table lamp, François-Xavier Lalanne, 1992 by SIAE 2023; set of candlesticks, Robert Goossens, 1970s by SIAE 2023; carpet, Diurne, 2022; *Poltrona Alta* armchair, Oscar Niemeyer, 1974 by SIAE 2023; floor lamp, Georges Jouve, 1955.
p. 157: dining table, George Nakashima, 1959; *055 Capitol Complex* dining chairs, Pierre Jeanneret, 1950s by SIAE 2023; *051 Capitol Complex* dining chairs, Pierre Jeanneret, 1950s by SIAE 2023; carpet, Diurne, 2022; cabinet, George Nakashima, 1961; *Cendrier Navette* ashtray, George Jouve, 1951.
pp. 158–159: *Terra Incognita* coffee table, Béatrice Serre, 2022 by SIAE 2023; *Pigeon* table lamp, François-Xavier Lalanne, 1992 by SIAE 2023; set of candlesticks, Robert Goossens, 1970s by SIAE 2023; carpet, Diurne, 2022; *Poltrona Alta* armchair, Oscar Niemeyer, 1974 by SIAE 2023; floor lamp, Georges Jouve, 1955; stool, Mercier Perriand, 1949; Gavina Spa, *Digamma* armchairs, Ignazio Gardella; mirror, Robert Goossens, c. 1972 by SIAE 2023.

26 Avenue d'Iéna, Paris (France), 2023
pp. 160–165: © Gaëlle Le Boulicaut

Art & Design
p. 160: *Méditation* console, Hervé van der Straeten, 2019; mirror, Hervé van der Straeten, 2019; vitrail, Gregory Gatserelia, 2019.
p. 161: *Gem Forest* side table, Béatrice Serre, 2019 by SIAE 2023; Cassina, *053 Capitol Complex* lounge chair, Pierre Jeanneret, 2019 by SIAE 2023.
pp. 162–163: bench, The Great Design Disaster, 2022; table lamps, George Jouve, 1950s; *Girouettes*, sculptures, Philippe Hiquily, 2009 by SIAE 2023; *Mythologie du vide* totem, Monique Rozanès, 1985 by SIAE 2023; *Secret Haché* totem, Monique Rozanès, 2018 by SIAE 2023.
p. 164: *Cloud* (installation), Jacopo Foggini, 2020; *Jinshi Pink Jade* coffee table, Studio MVW, 2017.
p. 165: Edra, *Ella* chair, Jacopo Foggini, 2015; vanity console, Lara Bohinc, 2010.

HOSPITALITY INTERIORS

p. 166: *Lily's*, François al-Hajj Street, Beirut (Lebanon), 2017 © Marco Pinarelli
p. 169: © Anthony Fleyhan. **Art & Design:** *Cloud*, installation by Jacopo Foggini
pp. 170–171: © Spiro
pp. 172–173: *Balthus*, Minet el Hosn, Beirut (Lebanon), 2012. © Vicky Mokbel
pp. 174–175: *Celcius*, Downtown, Beirut (Lebanon), 2016. © Eva Szumilas
pp. 176–177: *Cocteau*, Downtown, Beirut (Lebanon), 2012. © Vicky Mokbel
pp. 178–179: *Le Sushi Bar*, Minet el Hosn, Beirut (Lebanon), 2019. © Georges Zeydan. **Art & Design:** ceramics by Hala Matta (Nakima Atelier)
pp. 180–181: Quartier Chic, Minet el Hosn, Beirut (Lebanon), 2018. © Eva Szumilas – Illustrations by Cynthia Merhej
pp. 182–183: *Seray*, Downtown, Beirut (Lebanon), 2017. © Eva Szumilas
pp. 184–185: *Society Bistrot and Wine Bar*, Saifi, Beirut (Lebanon), 2012. © Joe Kesrouani. **Art & Design:** installation by Lara Khoury
pp. 186–189: *Spine*, Building Naccache Seaside Road (Lebanon), 2018. © Eva Szumilas
p. 190: View of southern hillside of Achrafieh, taken in Achrafieh, Beirut (Lebanon), 2019. © Ieva Saudargaitė
p. 191: *Spine*, Building Naccache Seaside Road (Lebanon), 2018. © Eva Szumilas
pp. 192–193: *Anu*, Nabu Museum, El Heri Seaside (Lebanon), 2022. © Eva Szumilas. **Art & Design:** tree by Eva Szumilas
pp. 194–195: *Aï Restaurant*, Vienna (Austria), 2017. © Walter Luttenberger
pp. 196–197: *L'Atelier de Joël Robuchon*, DIFC, Dubai (UAE), 2020. © Michele Nastasi **Art & Design:** installation by Jacopo Foggini
pp. 198–199: *Nikki Beach Restaurant and Beach Club*, Jumeirah, Dubai (UAE), 2016. © Courtesy of Nikki Beach Restaurant and Beach Club, Jumeirah, Dubai (UAE)
Nikki Beach Hotel, Kosta, Porto Heli (Greece), 2014. © Courtesy of Nikki Beach Hotel, Kosta, Porto Heli, Greece
pp. 200–201: *Play*, The H Hotel, Sheikh Zayed Road, Dubai (UAE), 2015. © Courtesy Play, Dubai (UAE)
p. 203: Ceiling at *Aï Restaurant*, Vienna (Austria), 2017. ©Walter Luttenberger
pp. 204–205: Ceiling at *Lily's*, François al-Hajj Street, Beirut (Lebanon), 2017 © Marco Pinarelli
pp. 206–207: Ceiling at *Society Wine Bar*, Saifi, Beirut (Lebanon), 2012 © Joe Kesrouani
pp. 208–209: Ceiling at *Society Bistrot*, Saifi, Beirut (Lebanon), 2012 © Joe Kesrouani
pp. 210–211: Ceiling at *Play*, The H Hotel, Sheikh Zayed Road, Dubai (UAE), 2015 © Courtesy Play, Dubai, (UAE)
pp. 212–213: Structure of *Spine*, Building Naccache Seaside Road (Lebanon), 2018 © Pulse Production
pp. 214–215: Ceiling at *Seray*, Downtown, Beirut (Lebanon), 2017 © Eva Szumilas
p. 216: © Courtesy SMO Gallery Beirut photo archive
p. 219: © Francis Amiand. **Art & Design:** Installation *Breathing Wall*, Najla El Zein, 2013; handle by Gregory Gatserelia
p. 220: © Courtesy SMO Gallery Beirut photo archive. **Art & Design:** from left to right: works of art by Eva Szumilas, Hala Matta, Gregory Gatserelia, Georges Mohasseb, Najla El Zein, Karim Chaya
p. 221: © Courtesy SMO Gallery Beirut photo archive. **Art & Design:** *6302 Spoons*, Najla El Zein, 2014
p. 222: © Courtesy SMO Gallery Beirut photo archive
p. 223: © Courtesy SMO Gallery Beirut photo archive. **Art & Design:** from left to right: works of art by Eva Szumilas, Karim Chaya, Niko Koronis, Hala Matta, Najla El Zein, Bokja, Ranya Sarakbi
p. 225: © Courtesy SMO Gallery Beirut photo archive. **Art & Design:** *Banc des amoureux*, Ziad Antar, 2012
pp. 226, 227, 228: © Marella Bessone
p. 229: Extract of TGDD comics by Mila Monaghan

All images in the book were created with the permission of the homeowner and/or museum that had the space in their collection at the time of the photo shoot. Every effort has been made in good faith to trace the copyright holders and obtain permission to reproduce the artworks that appear in the spaces in this book. The Publisher may be contacted by entitled parties for any iconographic sources that have not been identified.

Acknowledgments

This initiative, in the last chapter of a life, enables us to realize in detail the hours, the nights, the anxieties, the disputes, the achievements, and sometimes the reward of a whole lifetime of work. Thanks to the involvement and devotion of my partner in life at this time, Joy Herro, who with her work, at times bothersome with her countless questions, was the moving spirit and energy behind this book.

Edited by
Federica Sala

Art Direction and Layout
Giulia Dolci

Distributed in English throughout the World
by Rizzoli International Publications Inc.
300 Park Avenue South
New York, NY 10010, USA

ISBN: 978-88-918373-6-3

2024 2025 2026 2027 / 10 9 8 7 6 5 4 3 2 1

First edition: March 2024

This volume was printed at
L.E.G.O. S.p.A., Vicenza
Printed in Italy

Visit us online:
Facebook.com/RizzoliNewYork
Twitter: @Rizzoli_Books
Instagram.com/RizzoliBooks
Pinterest.com/RizzoliBooks
Youtube.com/user/RizzoliNY
Issuu.com/Rizzoli

FSC www.fsc.org MIX Paper | Supporting responsible forestry FSC® C023419